THE LIBRARY OF
JAZZ
PIANO

Additional arrangements by Doug Gould.

ISBN: 978-1-78558-240-0

Visit Hal Leonard Online at
www.halleonard.com

Contact us:
Hal Leonard
7777 West Bluemound Road
Milwaukee, WI 53213
Email: info@halleonard.com

In Europe, contact:
Hal Leonard Europe Limited
42 Wigmore Street
Marylebone, London, W1U 2RY
Email: info@halleonardeurope.com

In Australia, contact:
Hal Leonard Australia Pty. Ltd.
4 Lentara Court
Cheltenham, Victoria, 3192 Australia
Email: info@halleonard.com.au

CONTENTS

Agua De Beber
(Drinking Water)

Words by Norman Gimbel
Music by Antonio Carlos Jobim

Ain't Misbehavin'

Words by Andy Razaf
Music by Thomas 'Fats' Waller & Harry Brooks

All The Things You Are

Words by Oscar Hammerstein II
Music by Jerome Kern

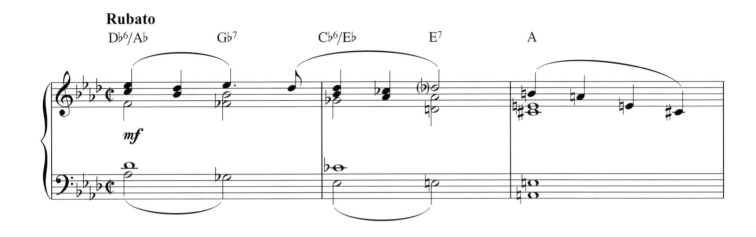

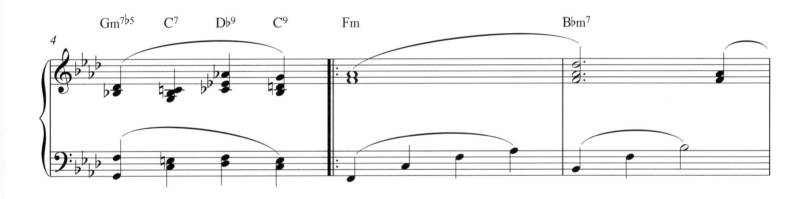

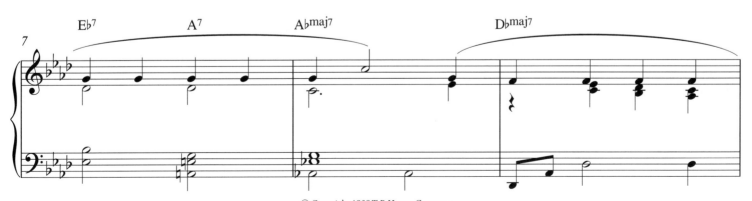

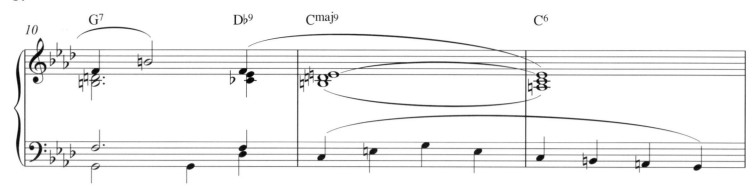

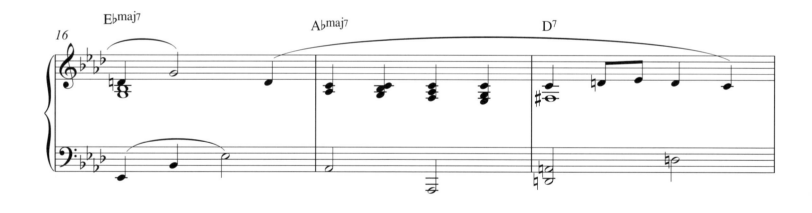

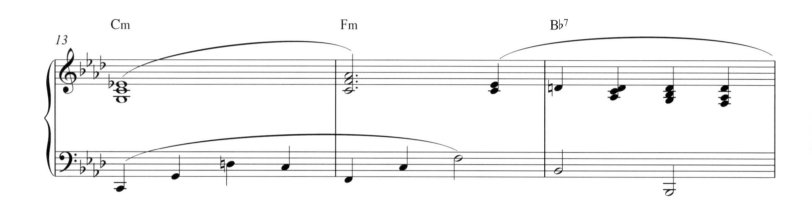

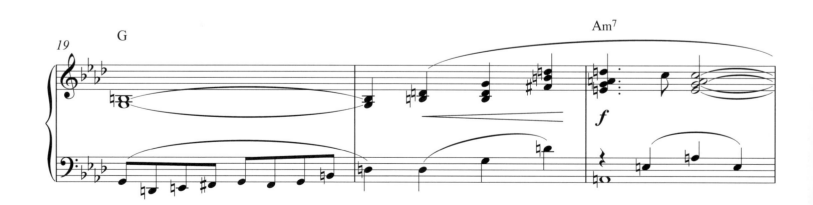

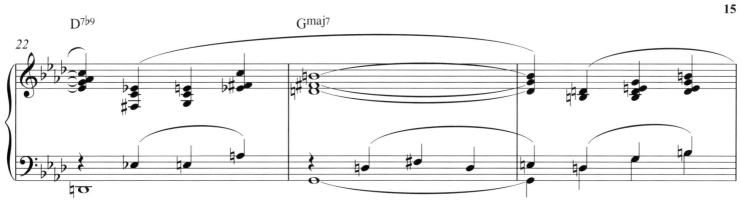

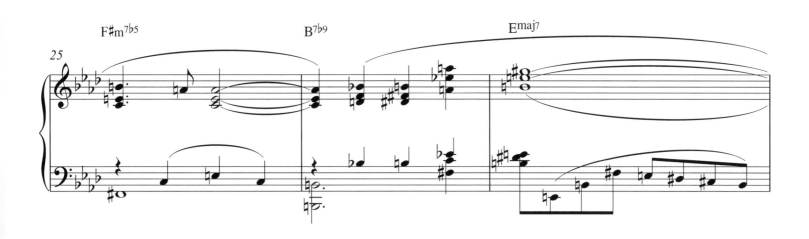

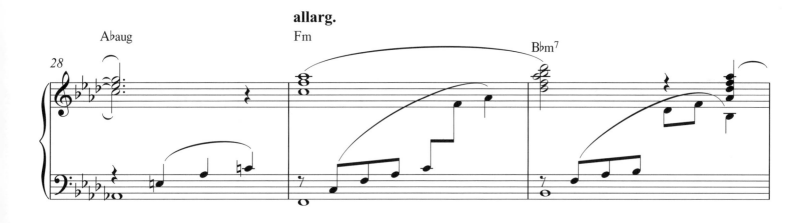

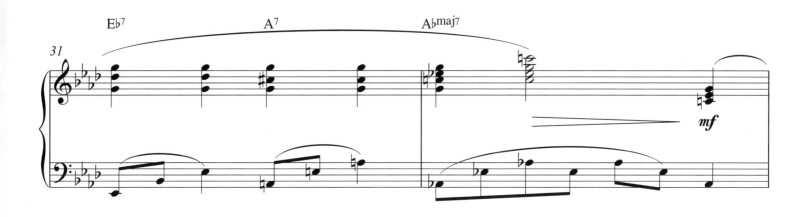

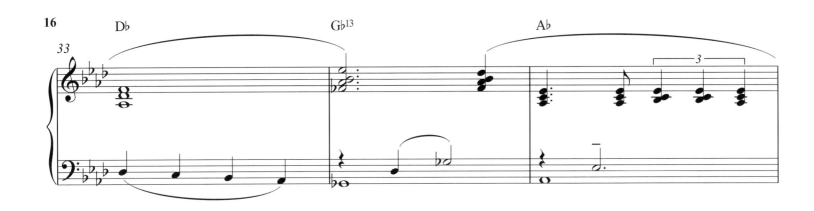

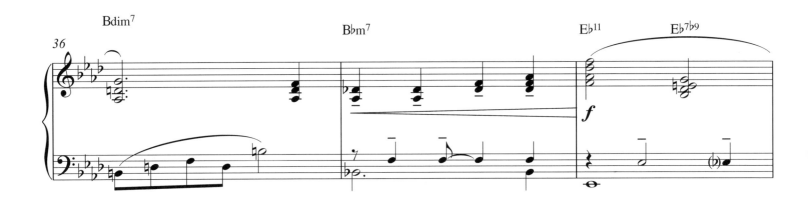

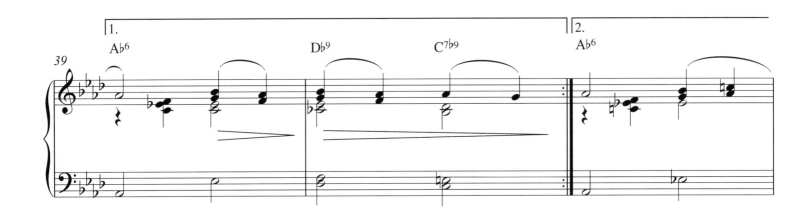

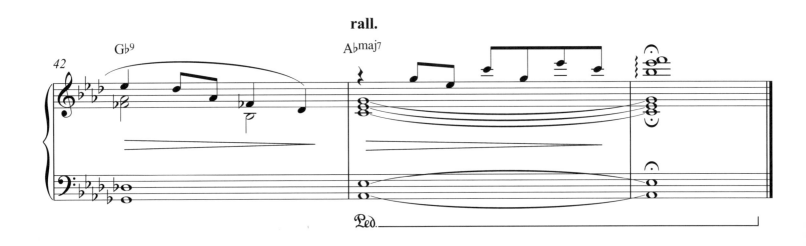

Alone Too Long

Words by Dorothy Fields
Music by Arthur Schwartz

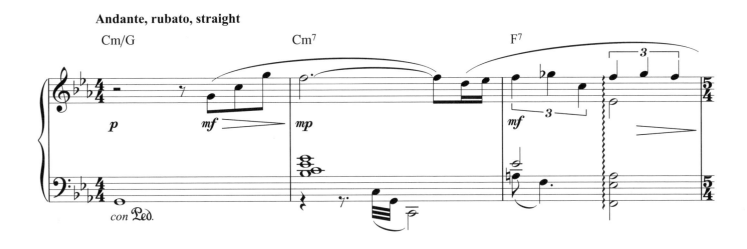

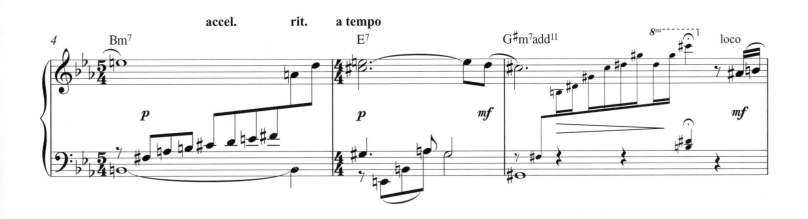

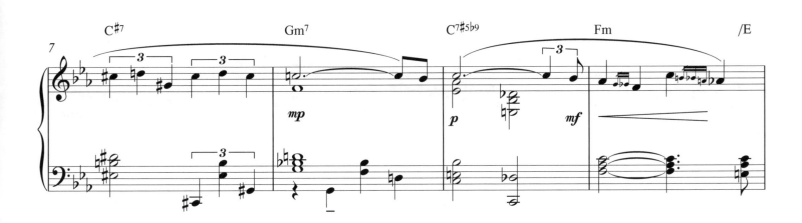

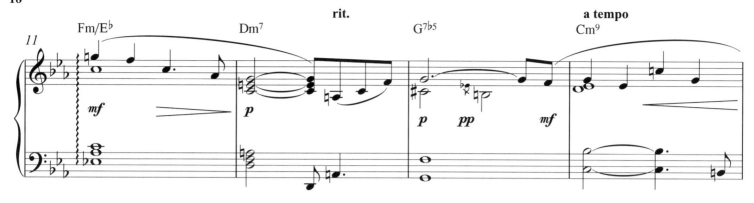

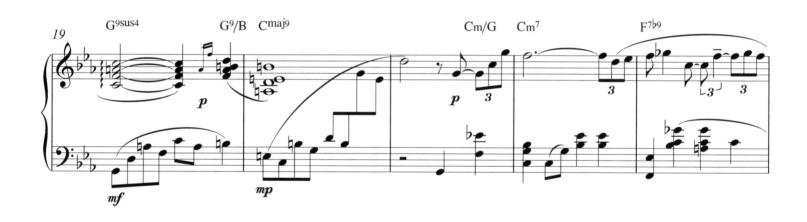

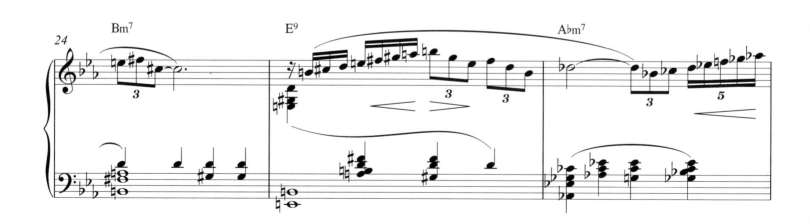

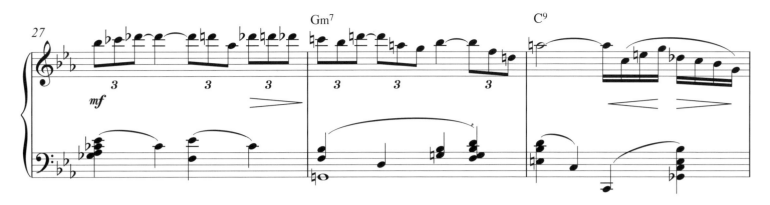

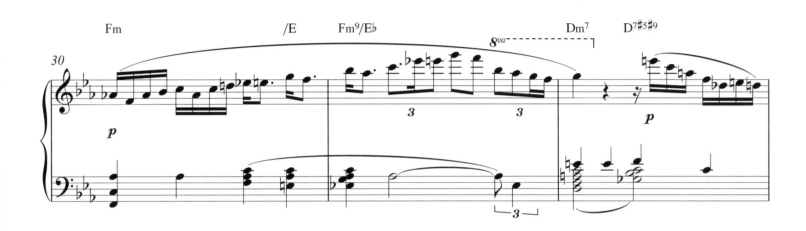

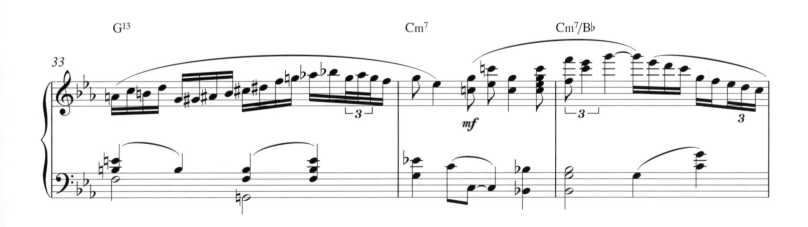

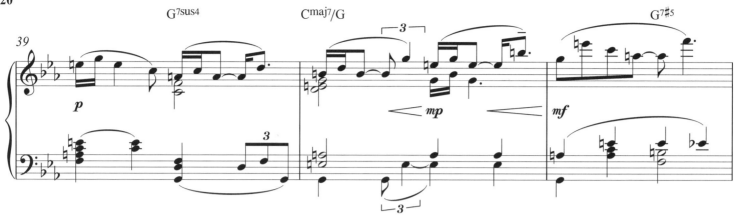

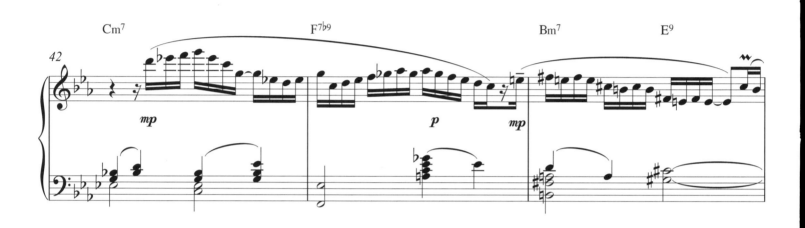

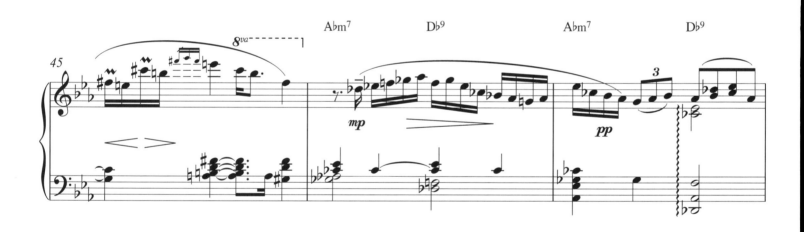

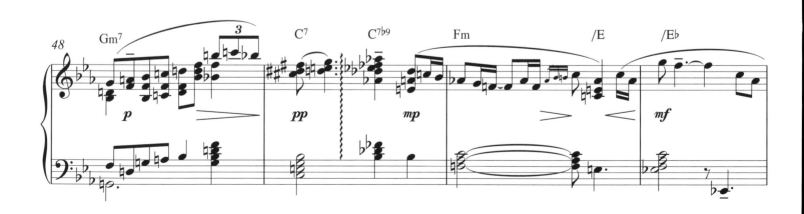

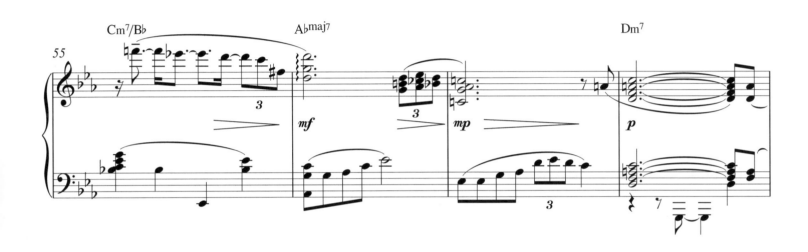

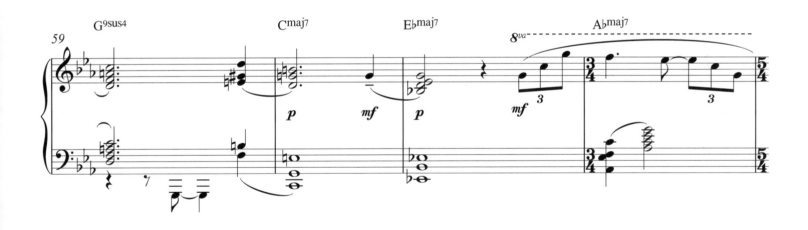

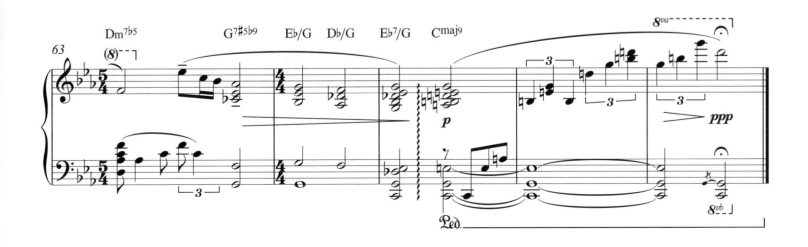

Anthropology

Music by Charlie Parker & Dizzy Gillespie

Moderate Bebop, swung

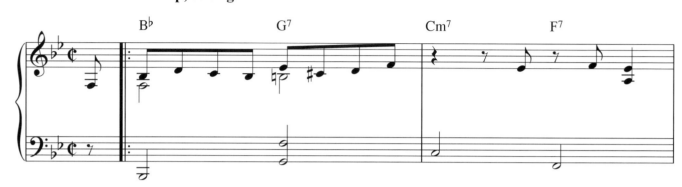

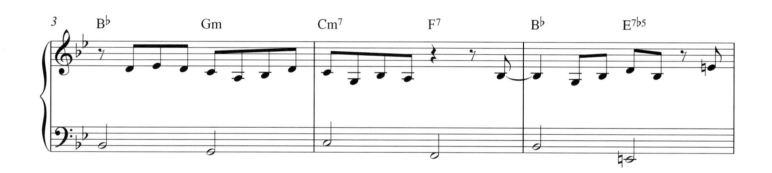

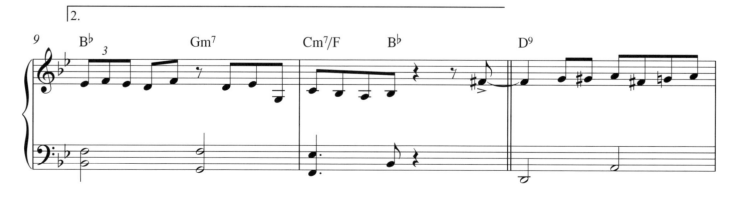

Basin Street Blues

Words & Music by Spencer Williams

Be My Love

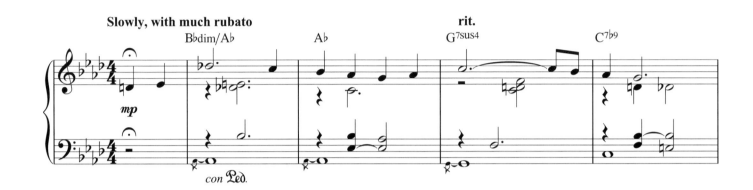

Words by Sammy Cahn
Music by Nicholas Brodszky

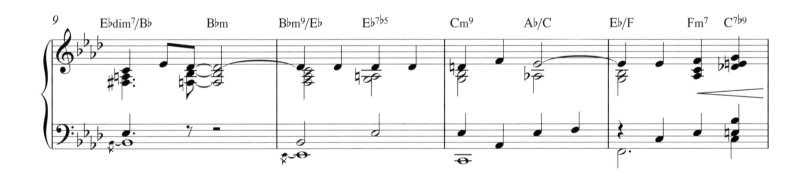

Black Coffee

Words & Music by Paul Francis Webster & Sonny Burke

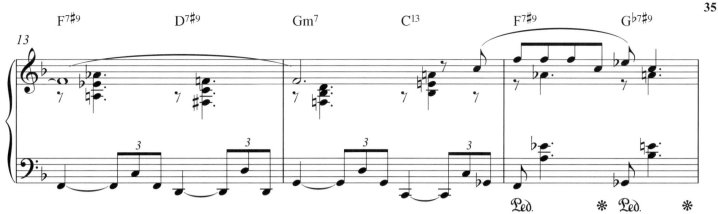

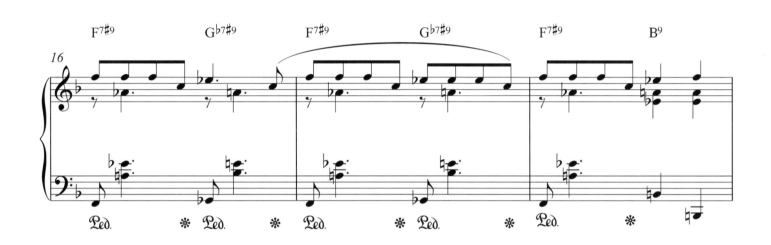

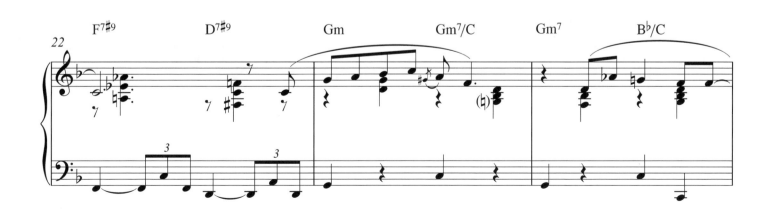

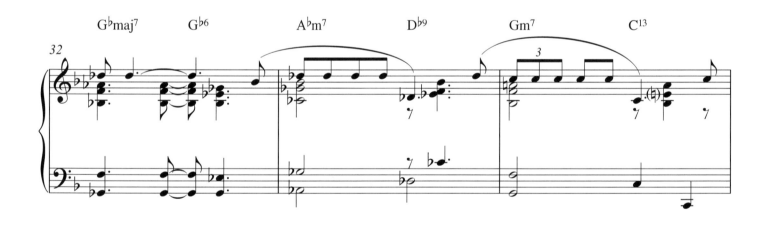

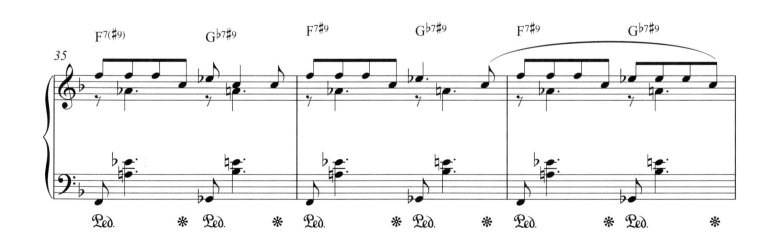

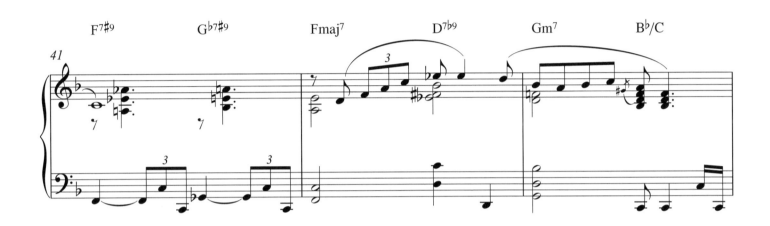

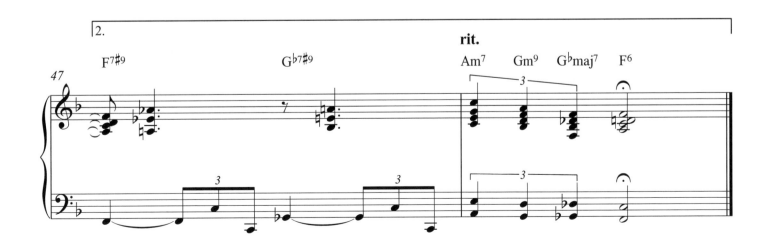

Can't Help Lovin' Dat Man

Music by Jerome Kern

Tempo di Blues (slowly), swung ♩ = 90

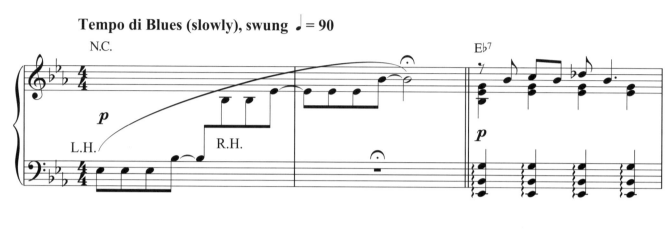

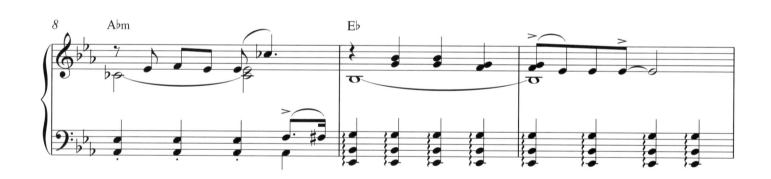

Cantaloupe Island

Music by Herbie Hancock

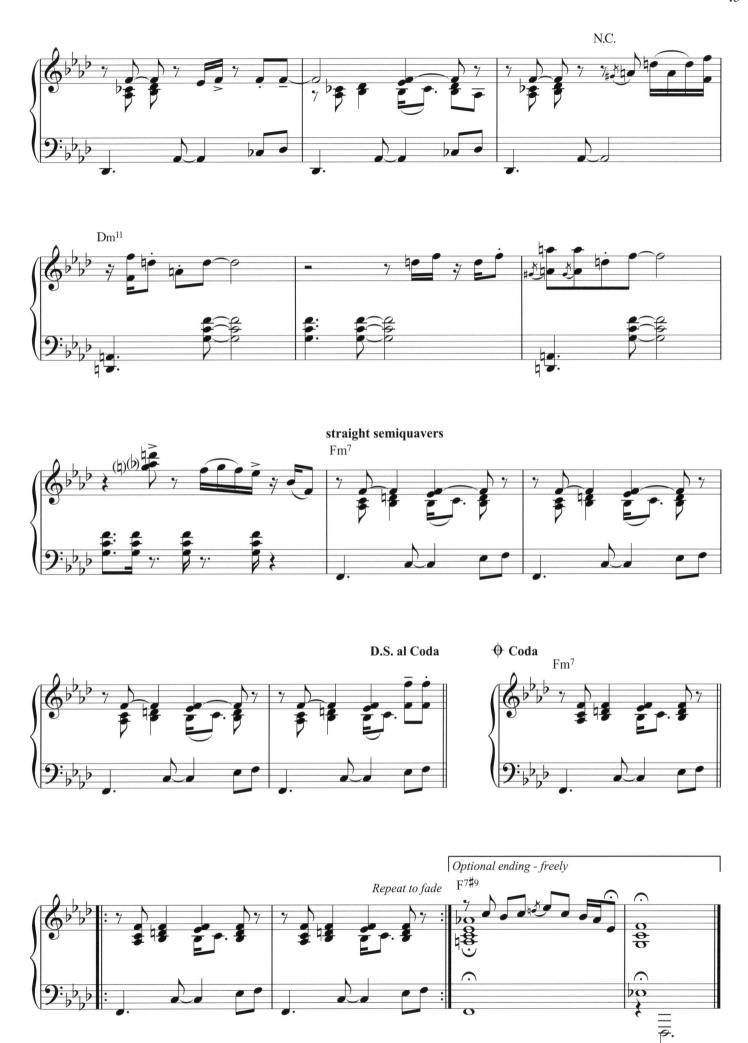

Chelsea Bridge

Music by Billy Strayhorn

Moderately, swung

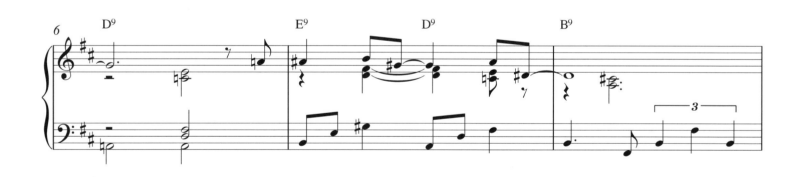

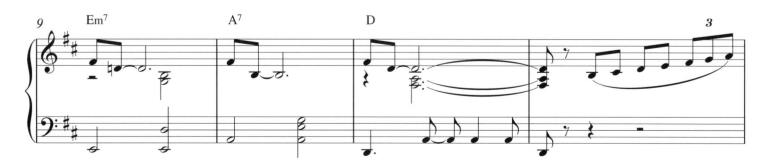

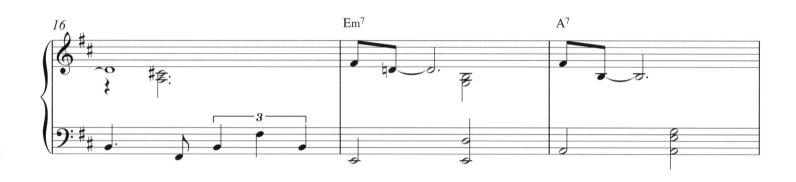

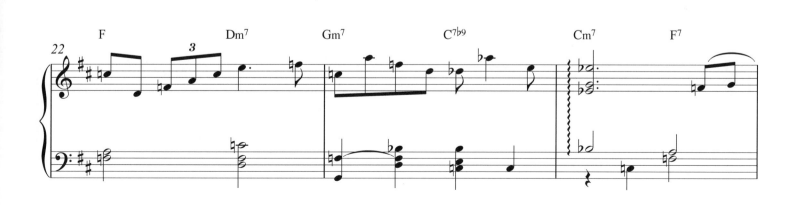

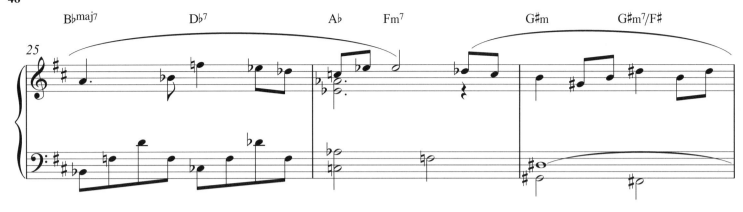

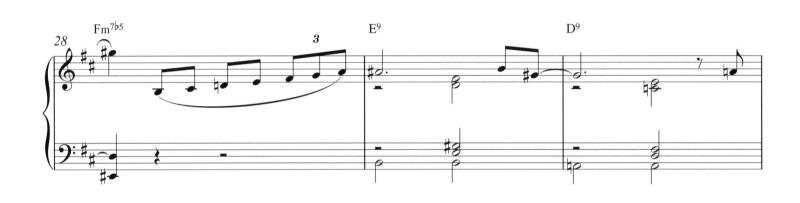

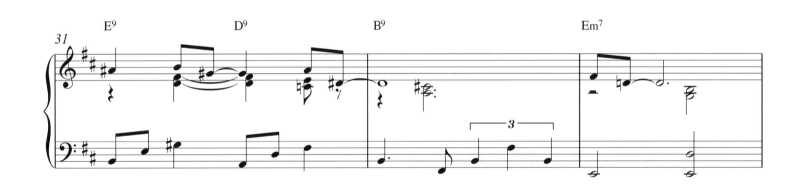

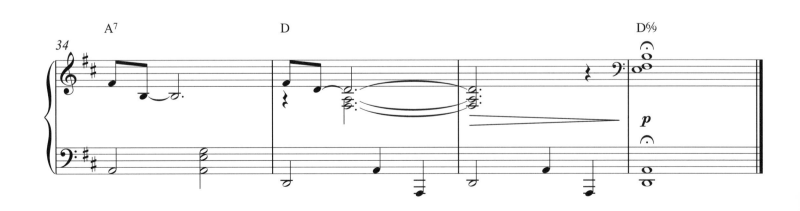

Corcovado

Words & Music by Antonio Jobim

Steadily and gently ♩ = 63

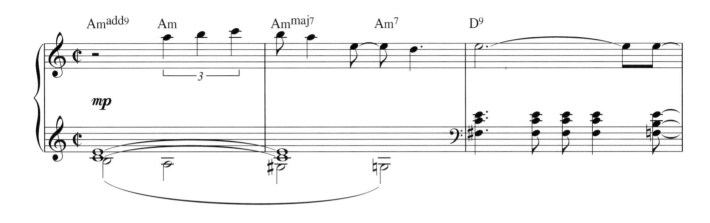

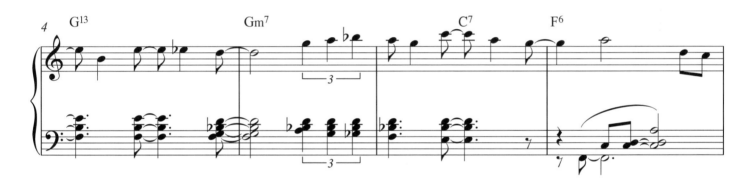

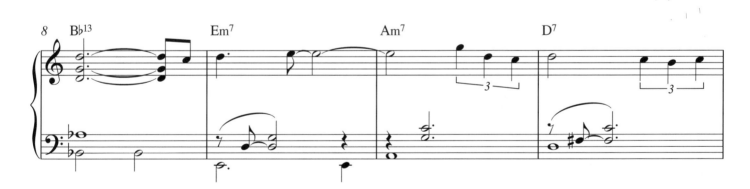

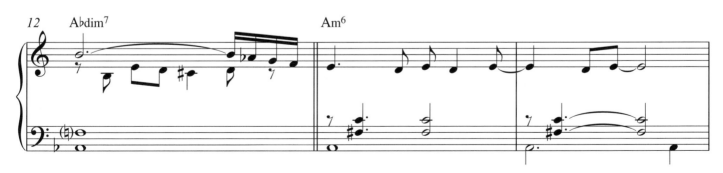

Desafinado

(Slightly Out Of Tune)

Words by Jon Hendricks, Newton Mendonca & Jessie Cavanaugh
Music by Antonio Carlos Jobim

Medium Bossa nova ♩ = 69

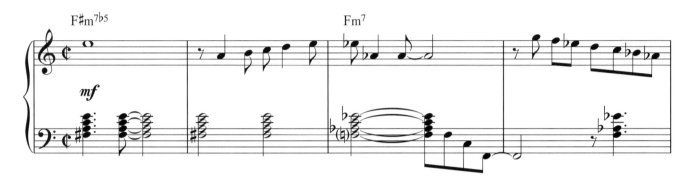

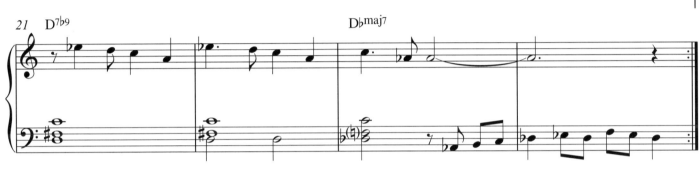

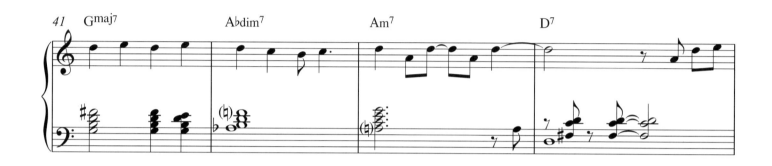

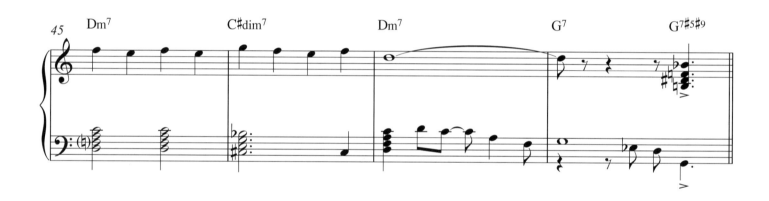

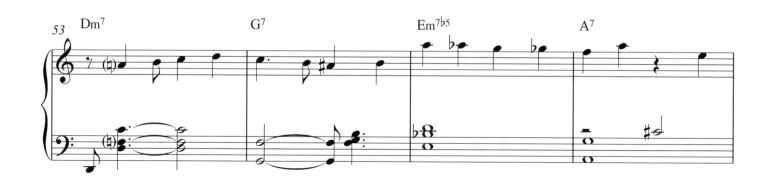

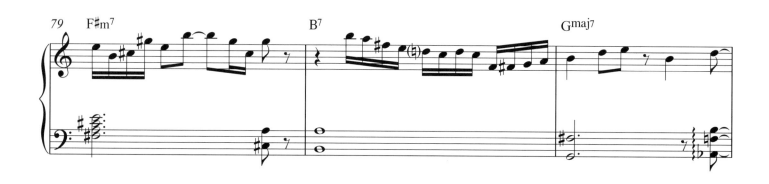

Don't Get Around Much Anymore

Words by Bob Russell
Music by Duke Ellington

Fly Me To The Moon

(In Other Words)

Words & Music by Bart Howard

Footprints

Music by Wayne Shorter

Medium swing ♩ = 154

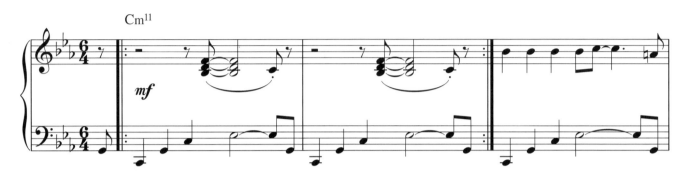

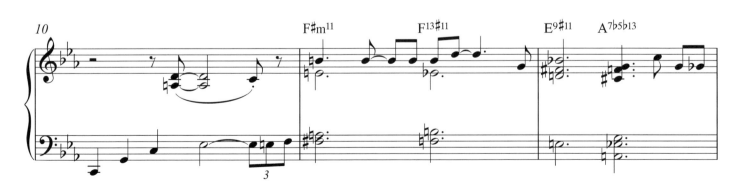

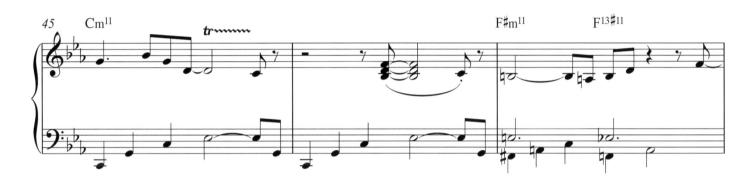

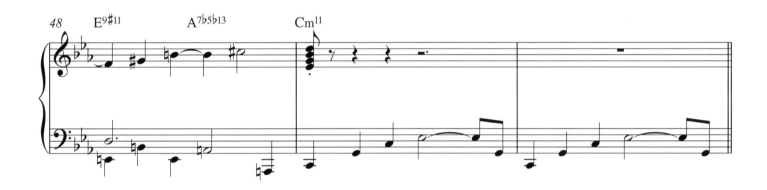

Frenesí

Music by Alberto Dominguez

(with a bounce)

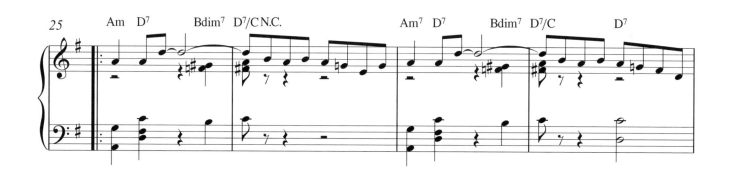

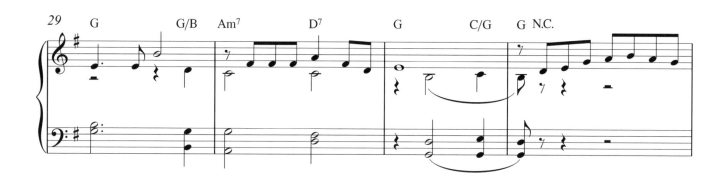

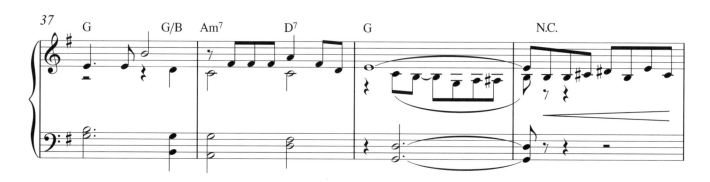

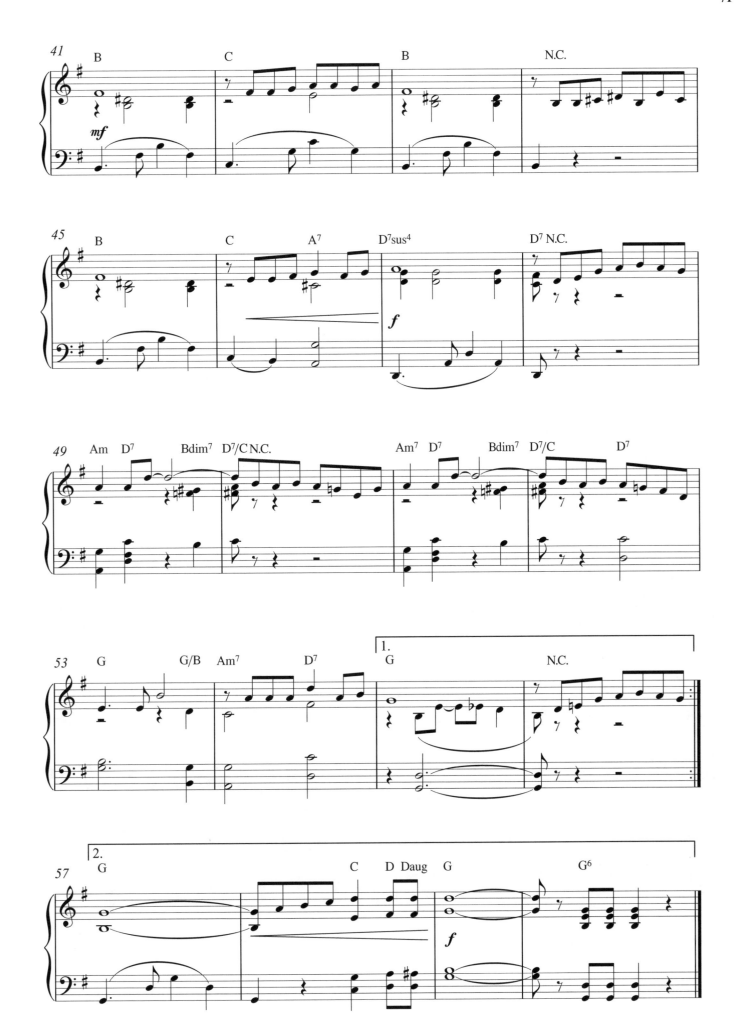

Georgia On My Mind

Words by Stuart Gorrell
Music by Hoagy Carmichael

The Girl From Ipanema

(Garota De Ipanema)

Words by Norman Gimbel & Vinicius De Moraes
Music by Antonio Carlos Jobim

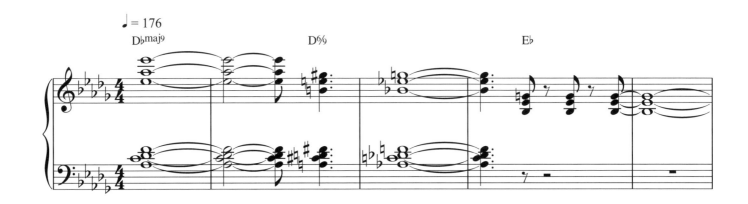

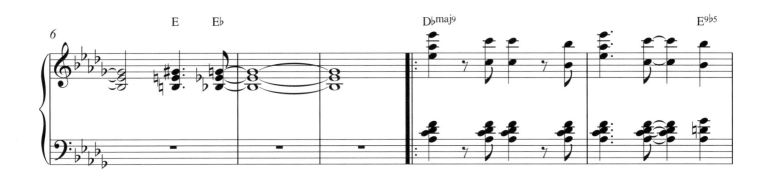

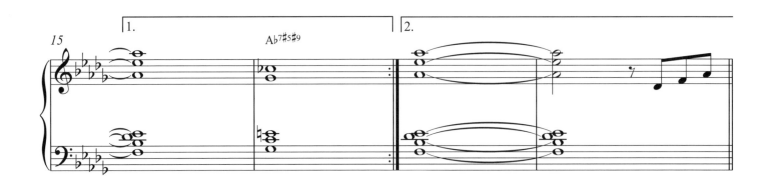

God Bless' The Child

Words & Music by Billie Holiday & Arthur Herzog Jr.

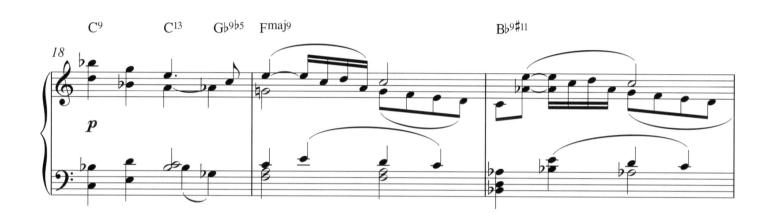

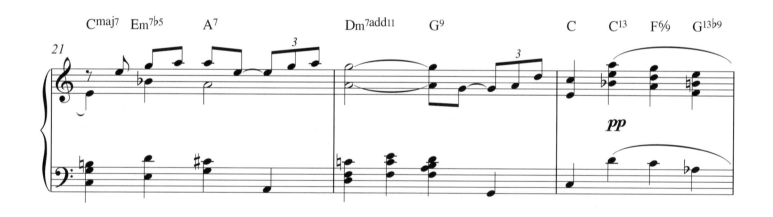

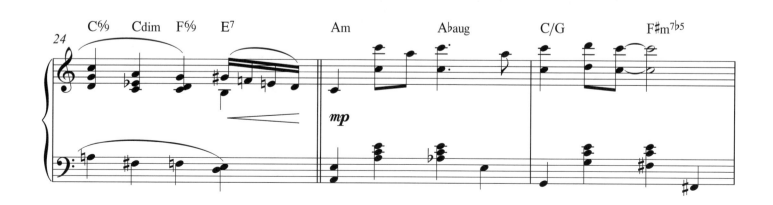

Handful Of Keys

Music by Thomas 'Fats' Waller

Honeysuckle Rose

Words by Andy Razaf
Music by Fats Waller

Moderately slow

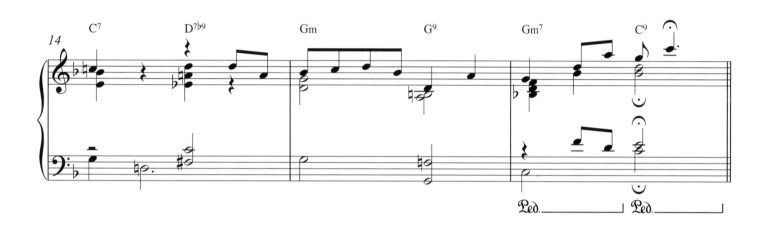

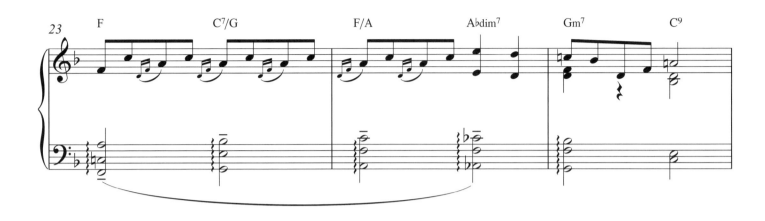

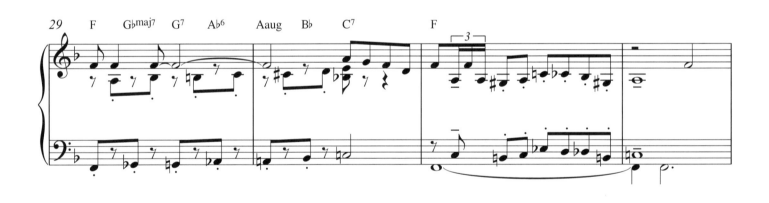

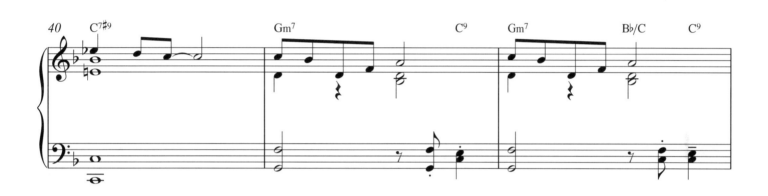

How Insensitive

Words by Vinicius De Moraes
Music by Antonio Carlos Jobim

In Your Own Sweet Way

Music by Dave Brubeck

Moderate

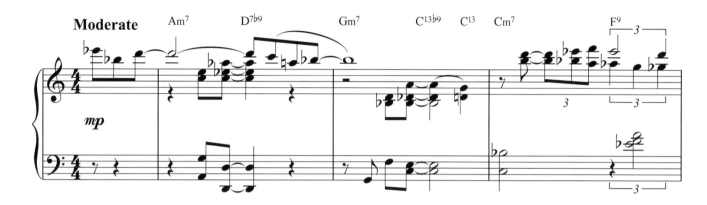

In the style of a waltz

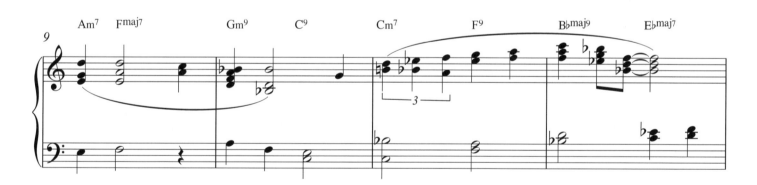

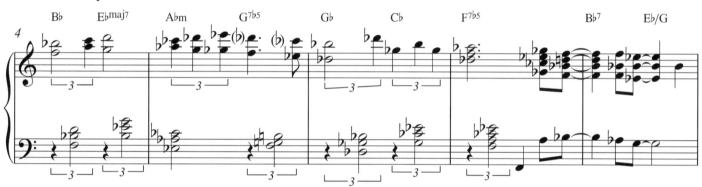

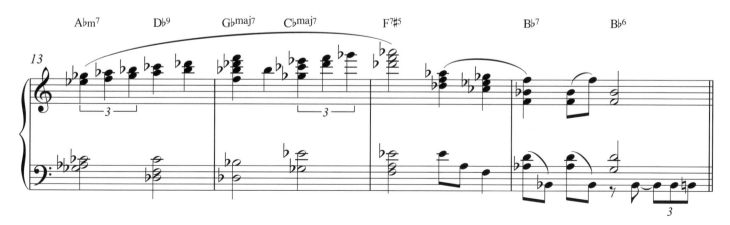

Easy swing

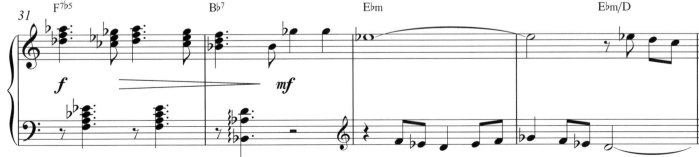

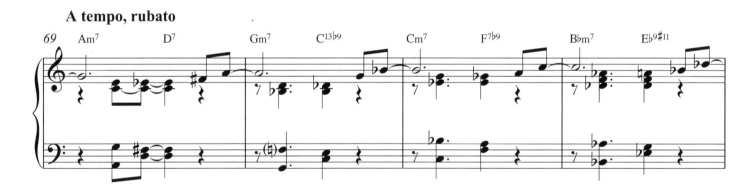

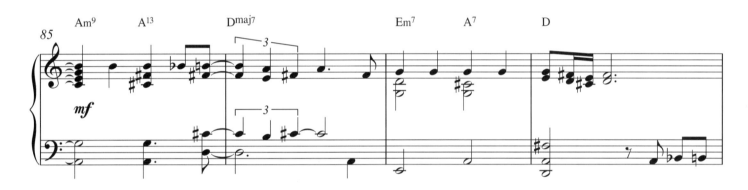

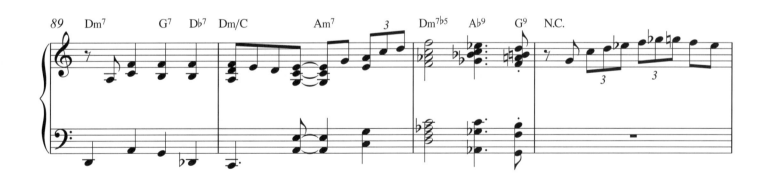

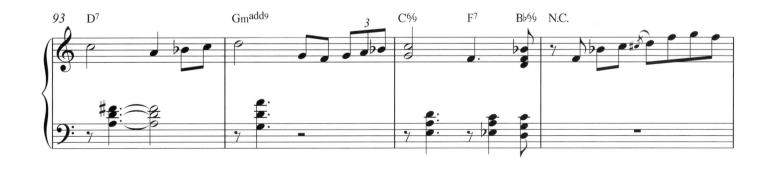

In the style of a waltz

It Might As Well Be Spring

Words by Oscar Hammerstein II
Music by Richard Rodgers

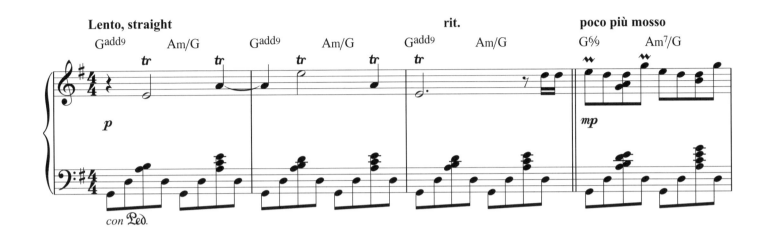

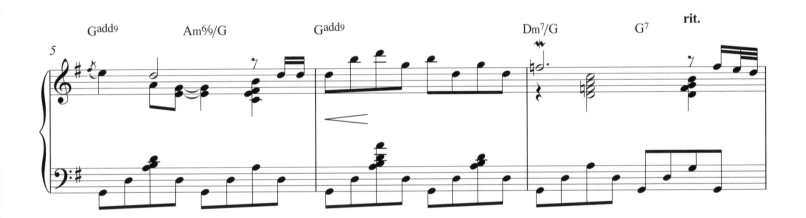

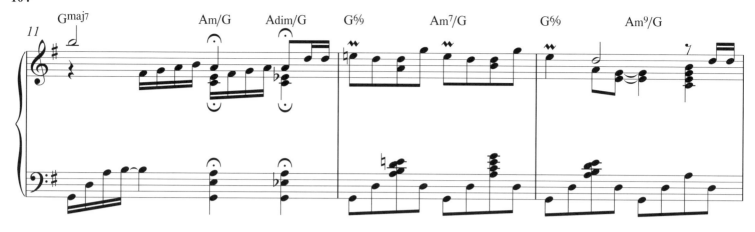

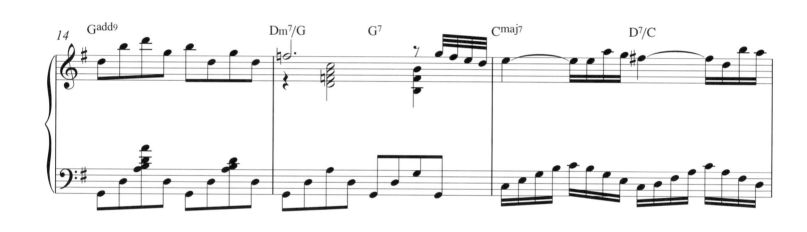

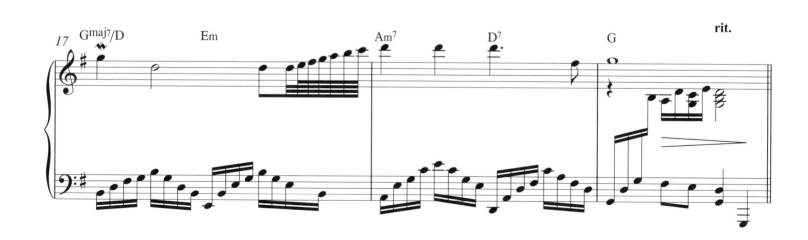

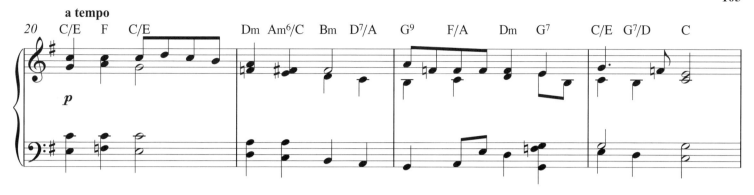

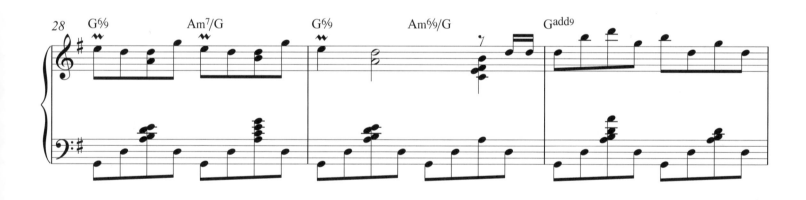

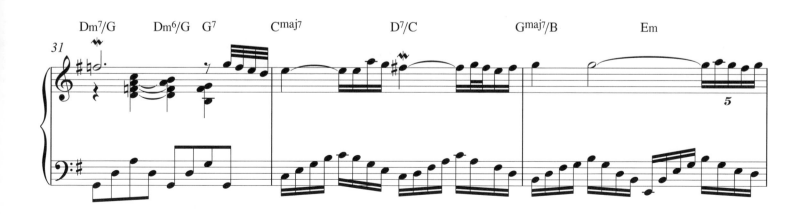

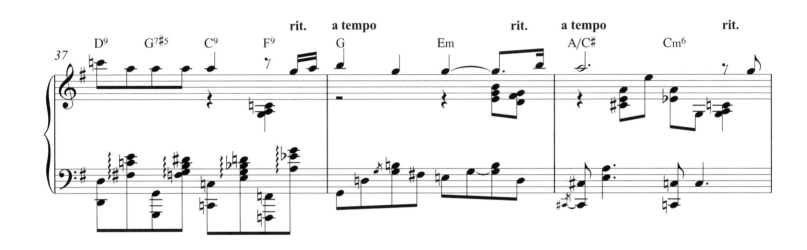

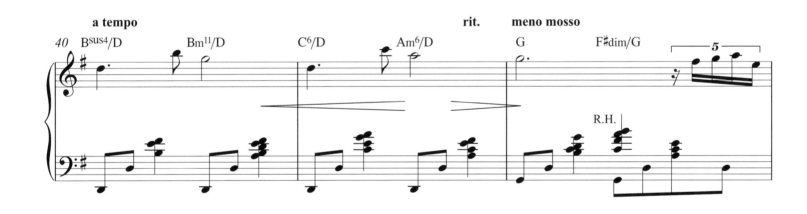

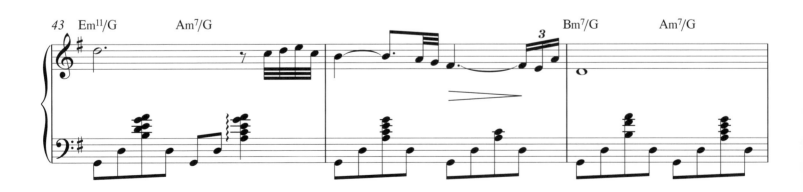

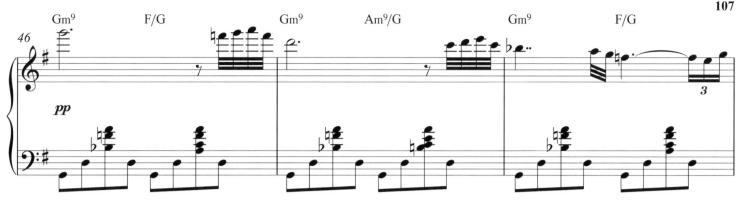

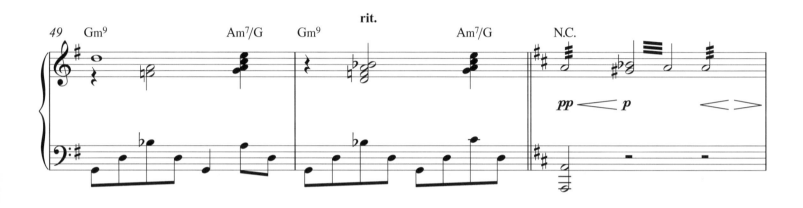

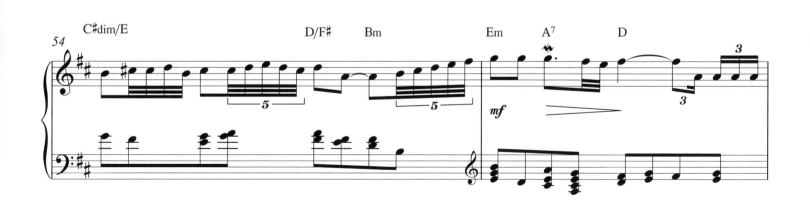

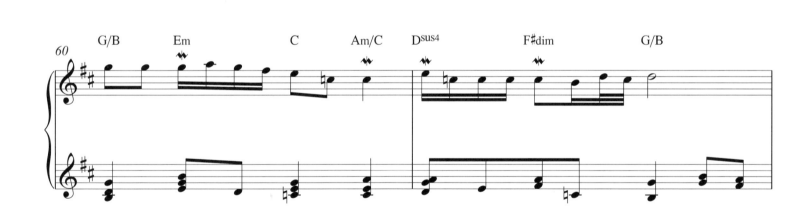

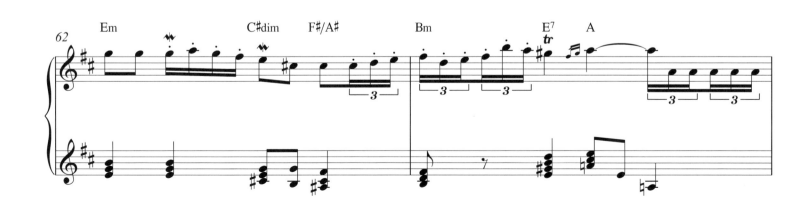

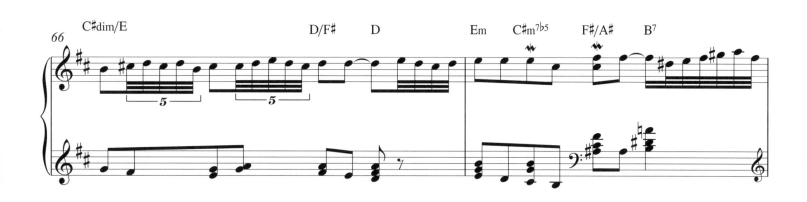

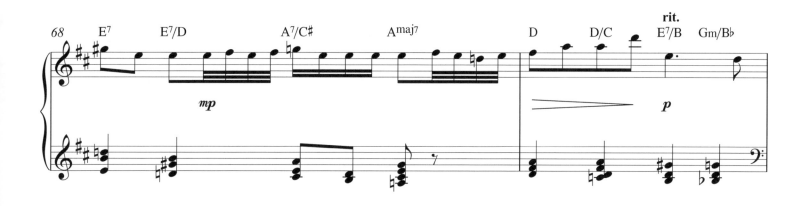

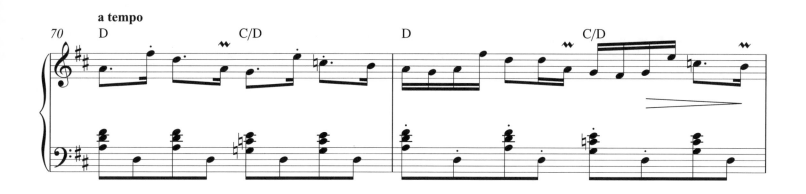

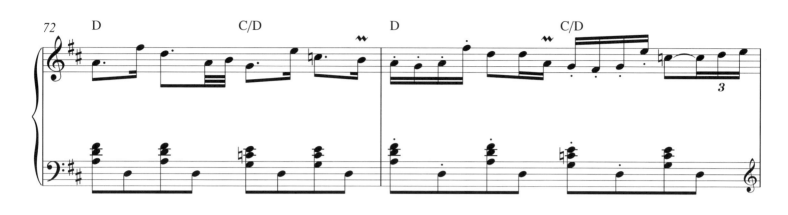

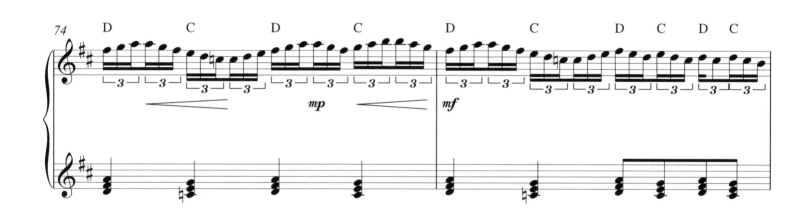

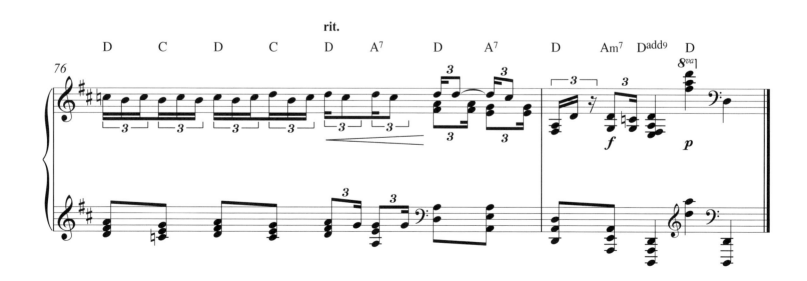

It Never Entered My Mind

Words by Lorenz Hart
Music by Richard Rodgers

112

Li'l Darlin'

Music by Neal Hefti

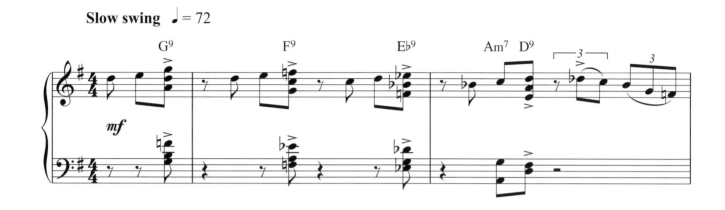

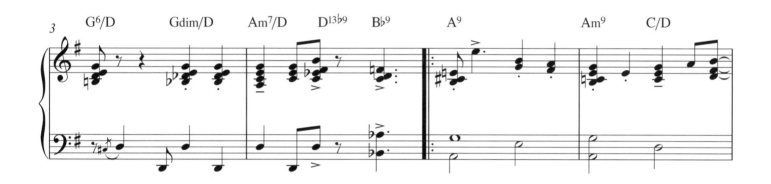

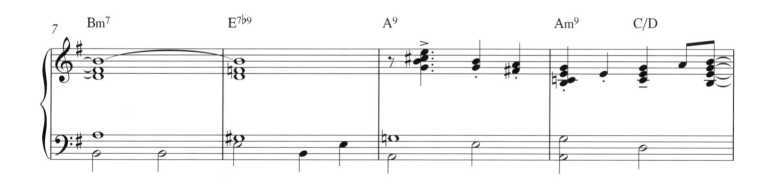

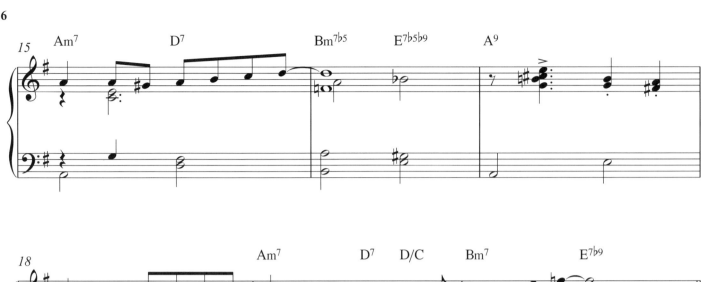

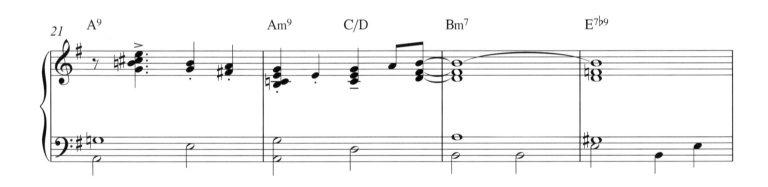

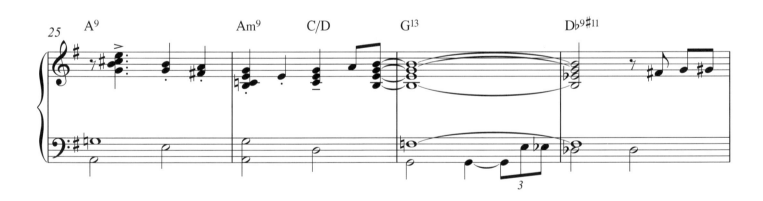

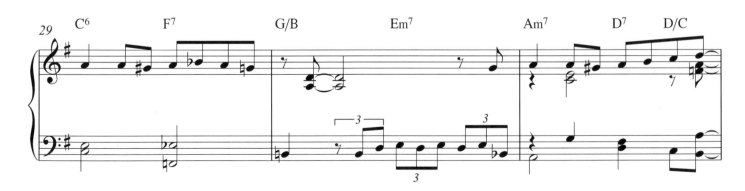

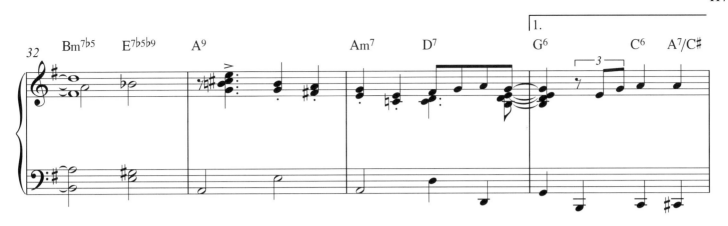

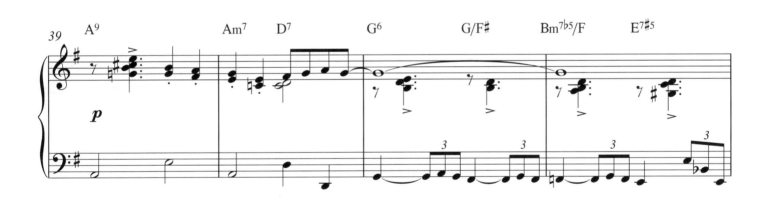

Love Theme From Spartacus

Words by Alex North & Terry Callier
Music by Terry Callier

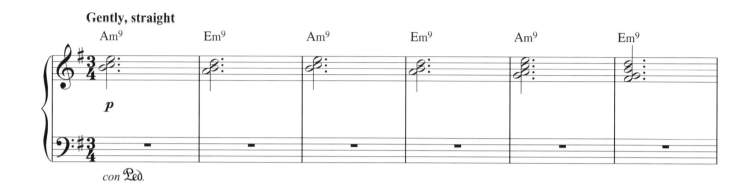

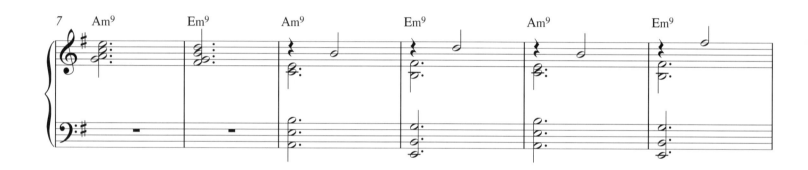

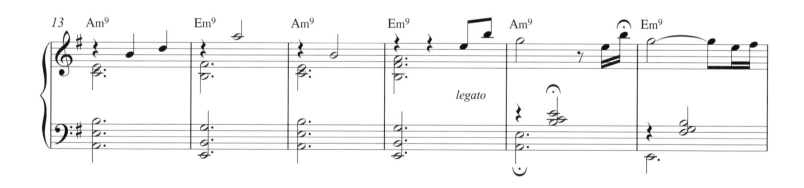

Lullaby Of Birdland

Words by George David Weiss
Music by George Shearing

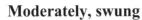

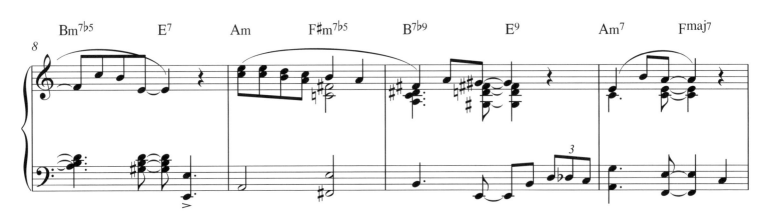

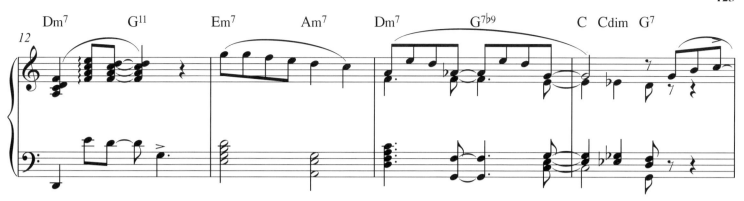

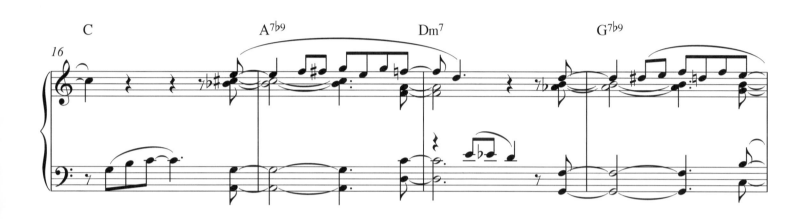

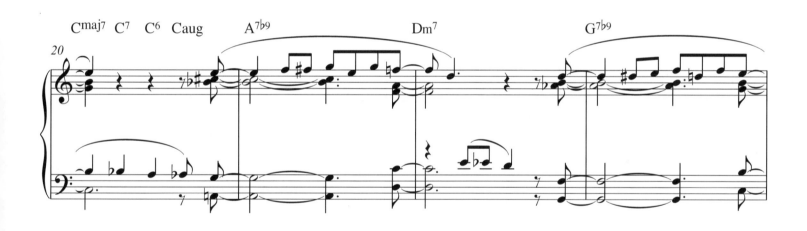

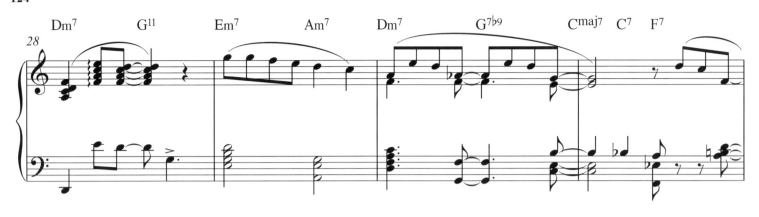

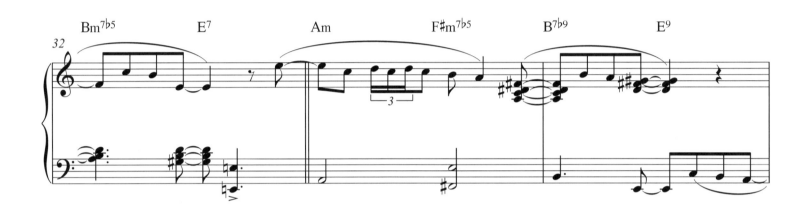

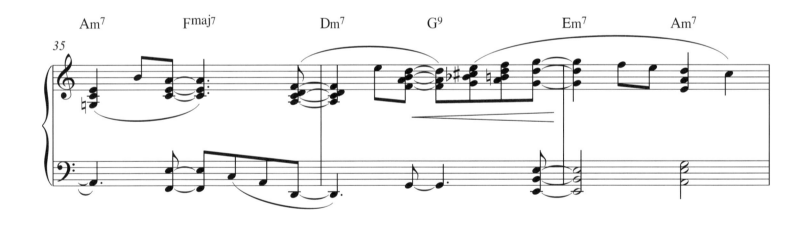

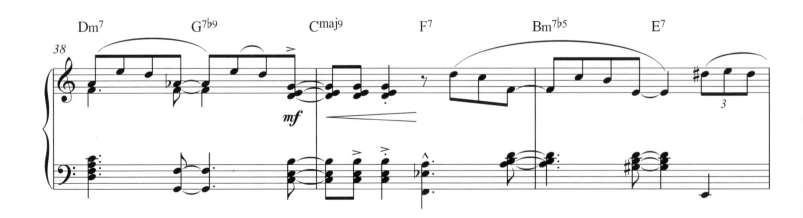

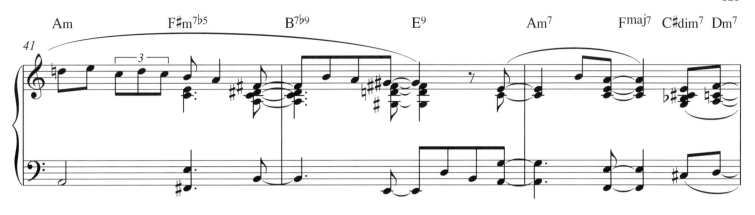

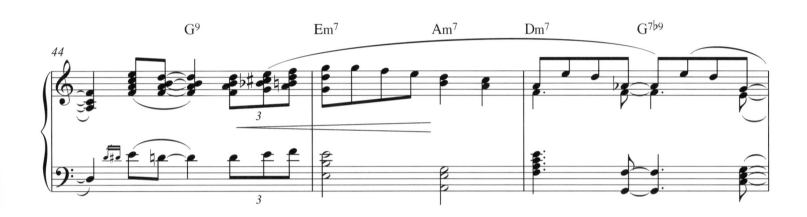

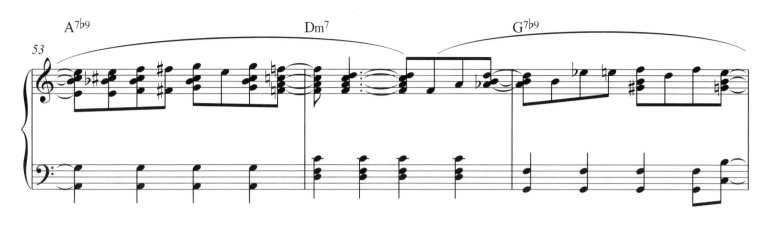

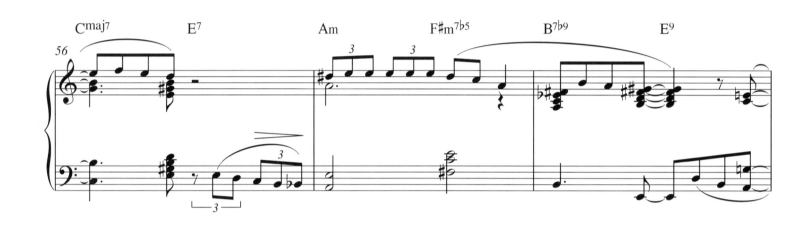

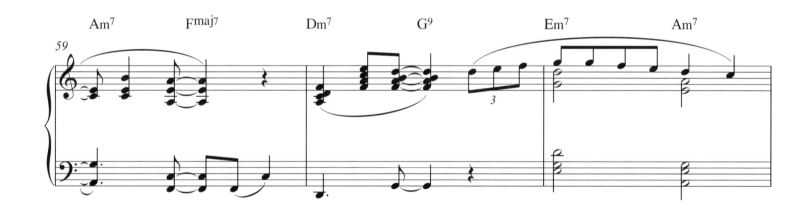

Lush Life

Words & Music by Billy Strayhorn

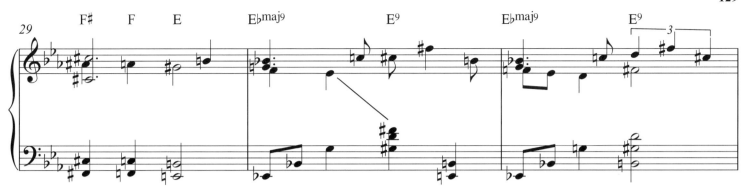

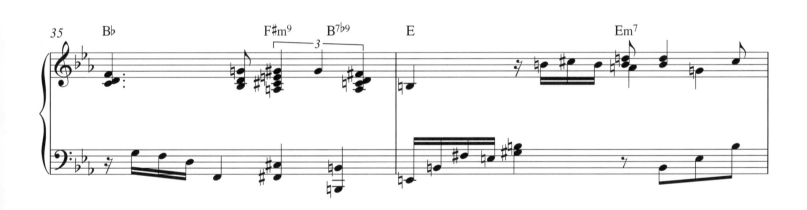

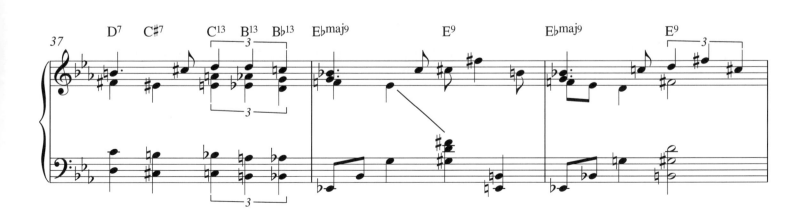

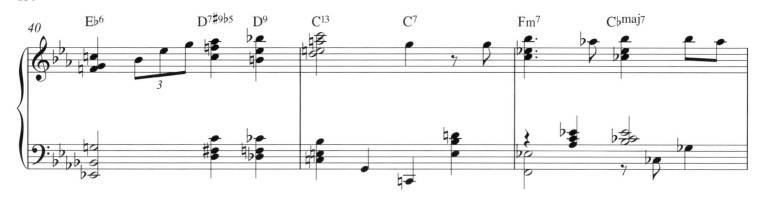

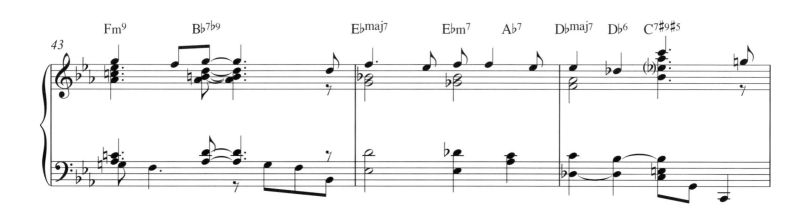

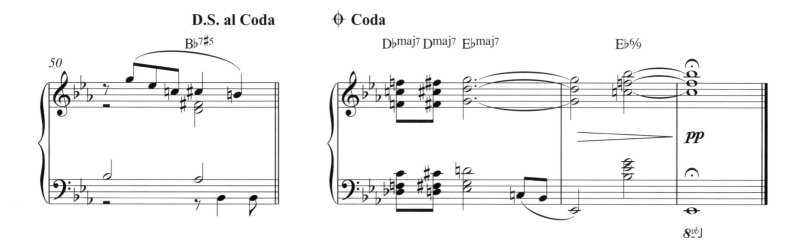

Maiden Voyage

Music by Herbie Hancock

Moderately ♩ = 118

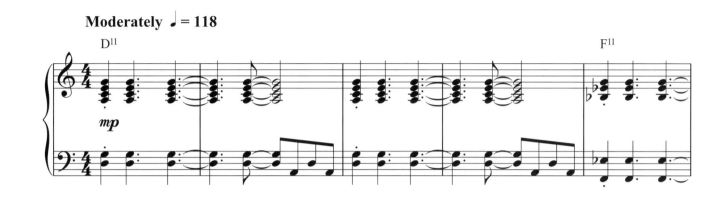

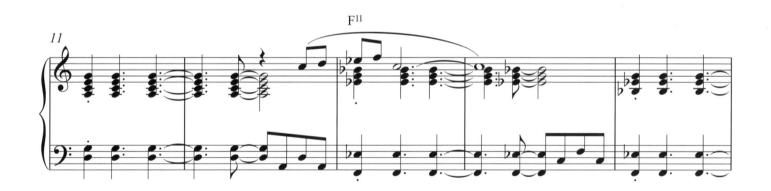

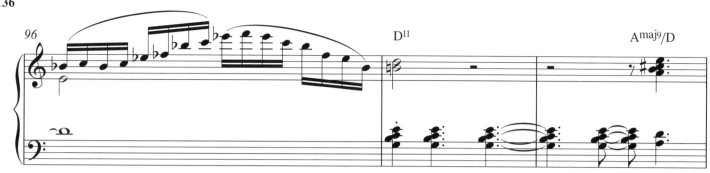

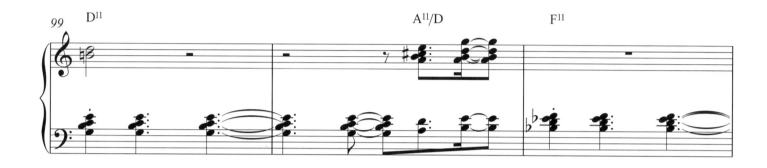

Mas Que Nada

(Say No More)

Words & Music by Jorge Ben

Misty

Words & Music by Erroll Garner & Johnny Burke

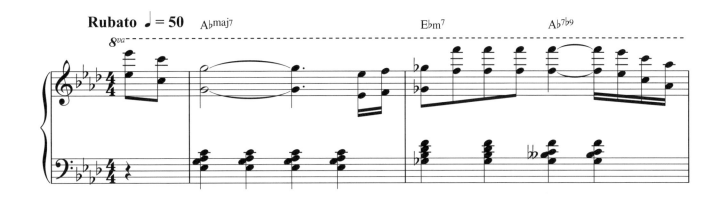

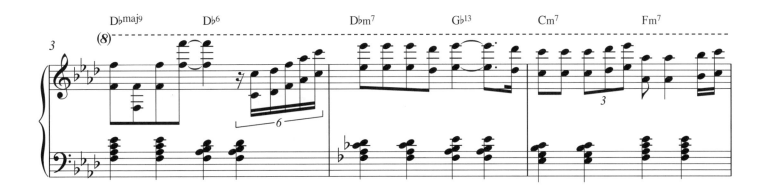

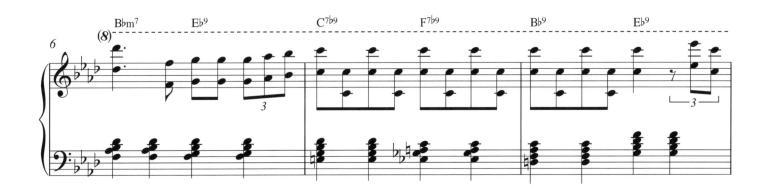

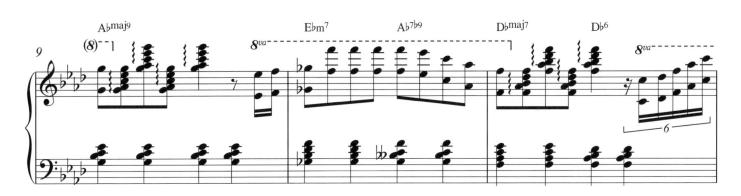

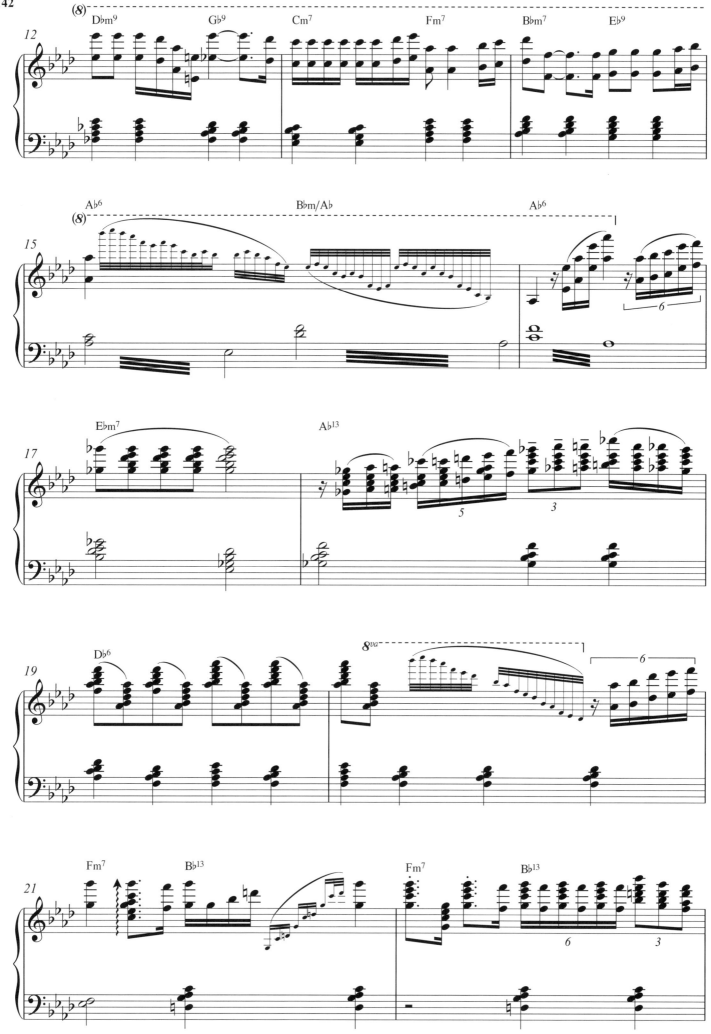

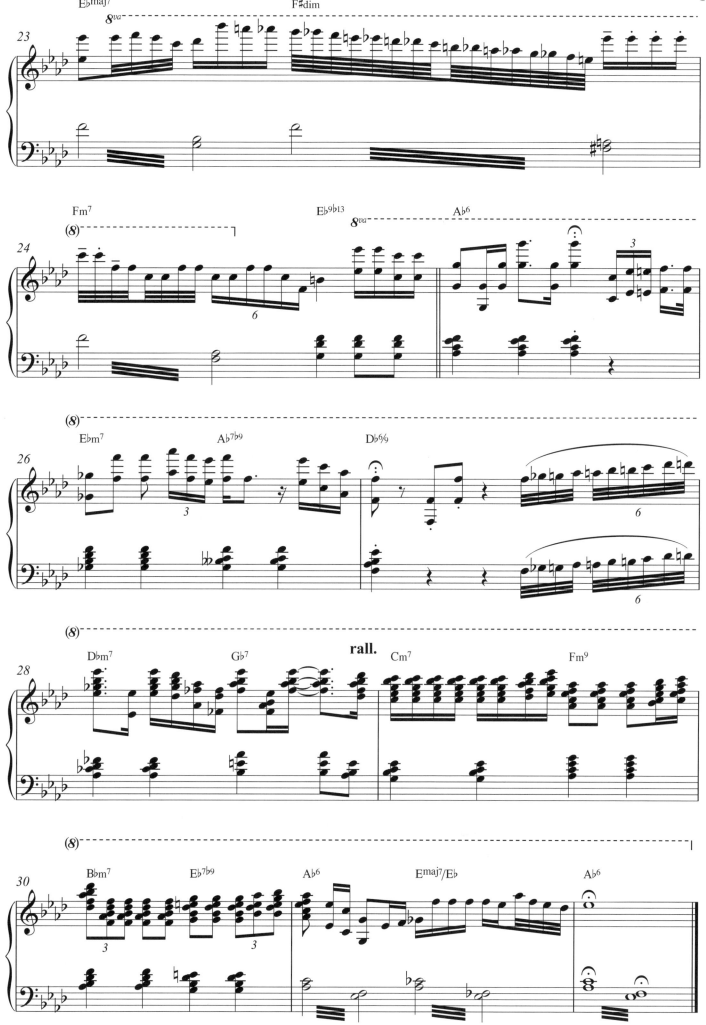

Mona Lisa

Words & Music by Jay Livingston & Ray Evans

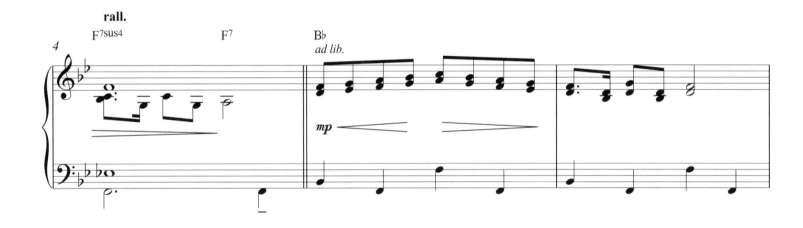

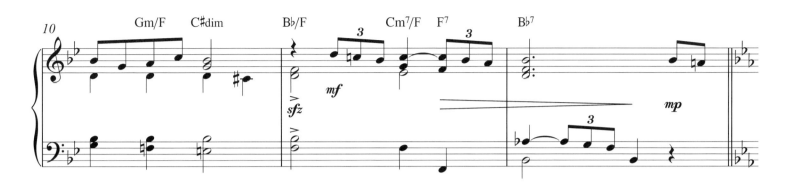

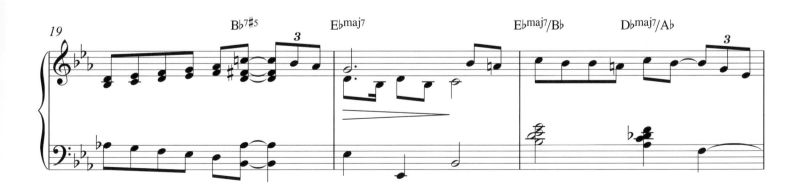

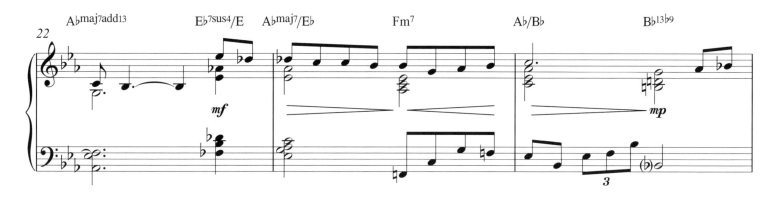

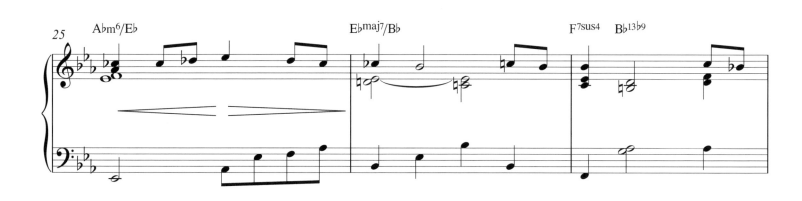

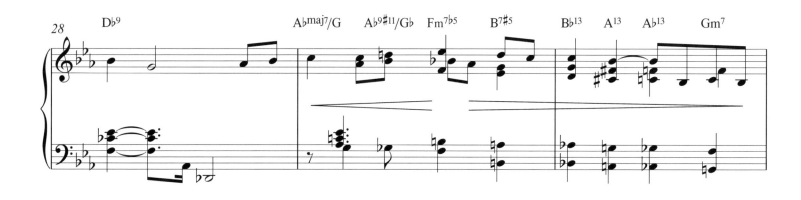

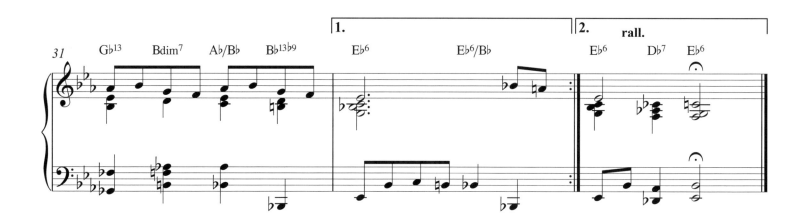

Monk's Mood

Music by Thelonious Monk

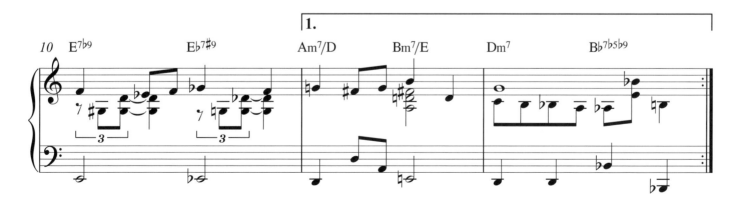

My Favorite Things

Words by Oscar Hammerstein II
Music by Richard Rodgers

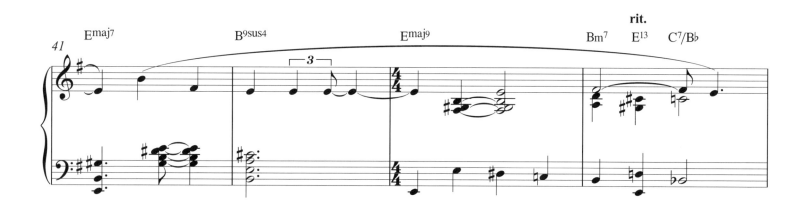

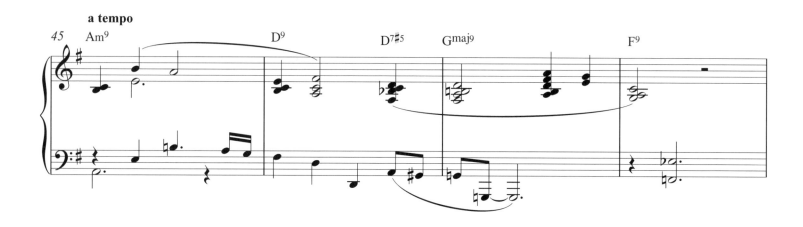

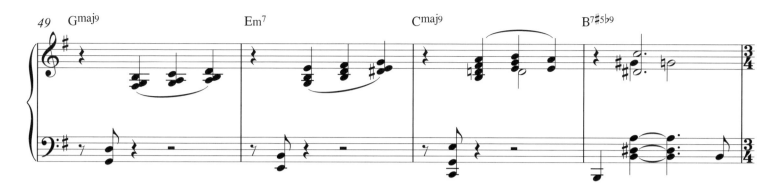

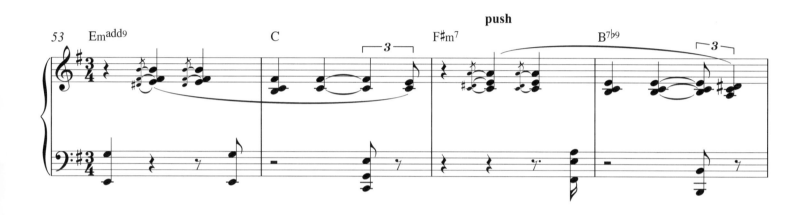

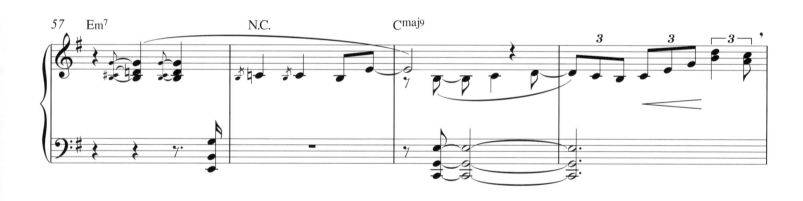

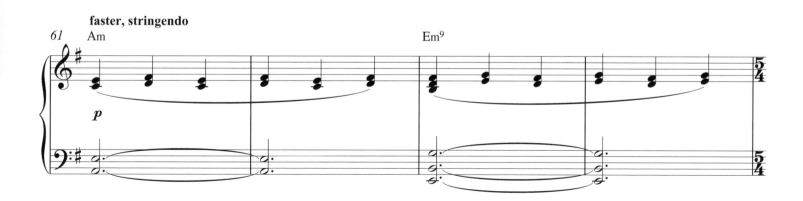

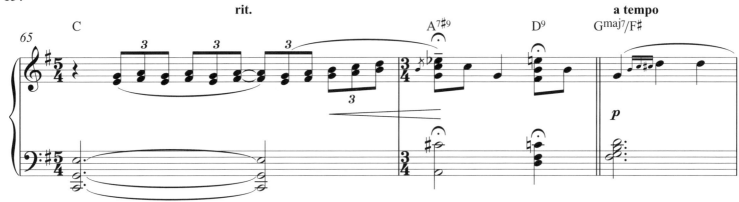

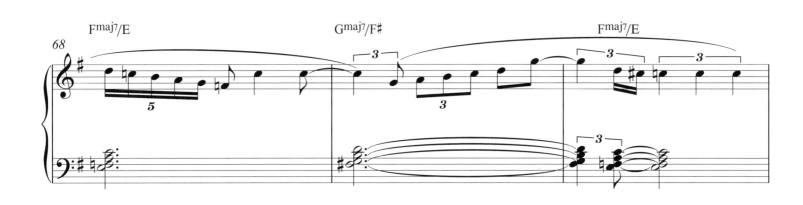

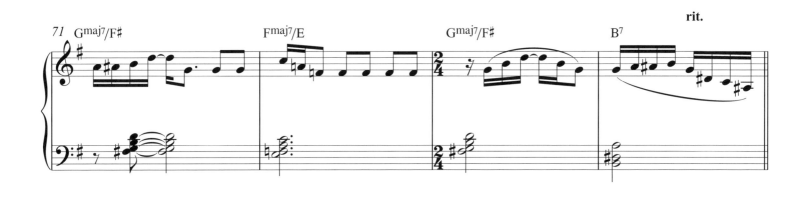

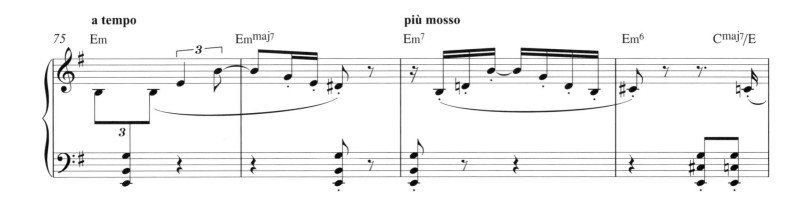

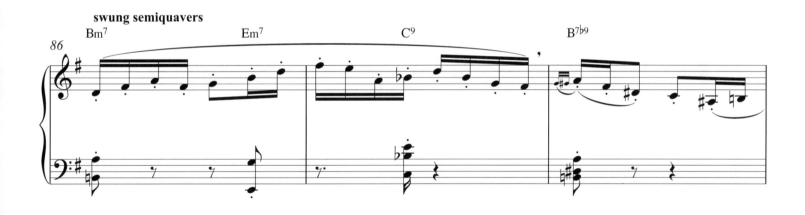

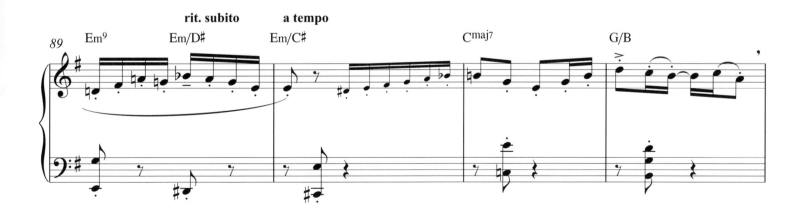

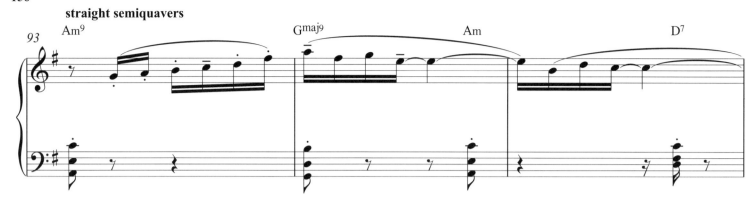

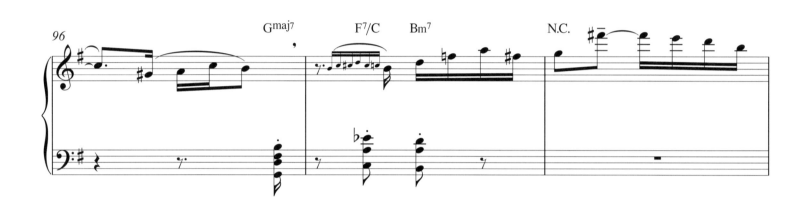

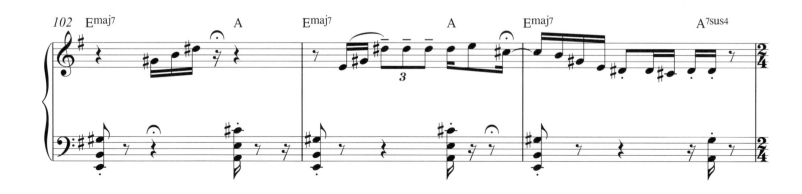

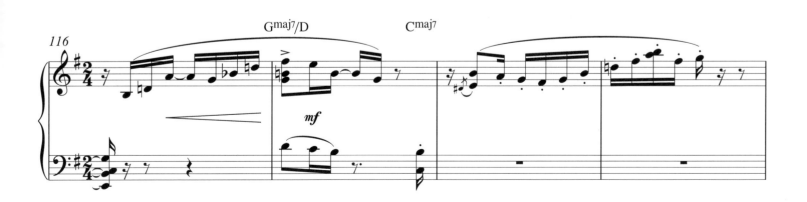

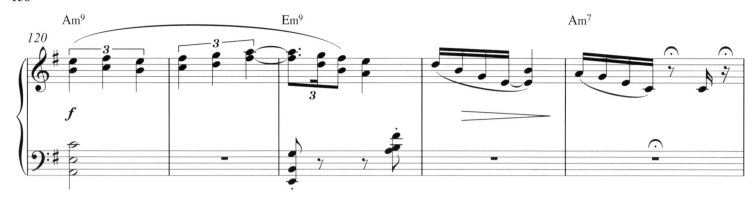

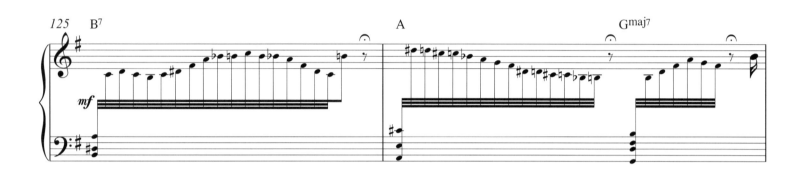

meno mosso, swung semiquavers

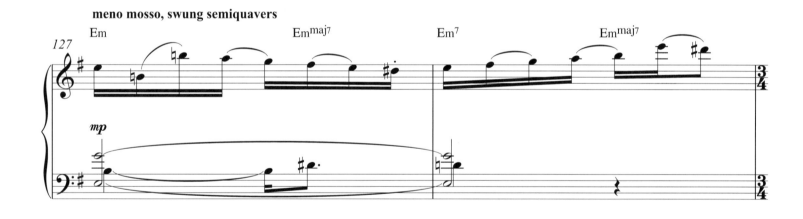

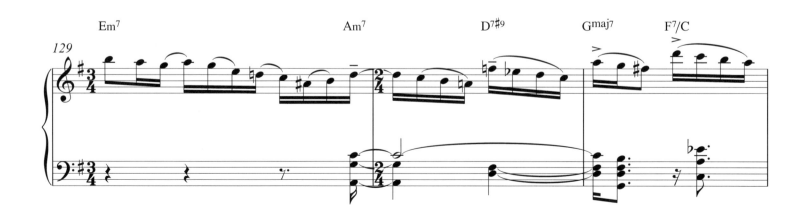

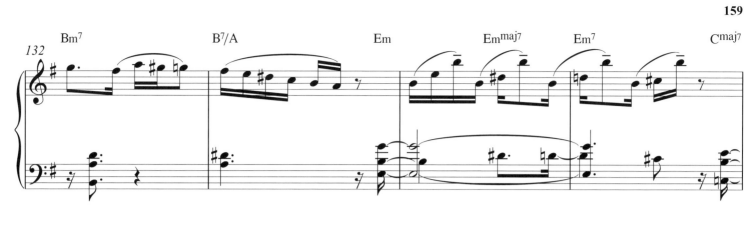

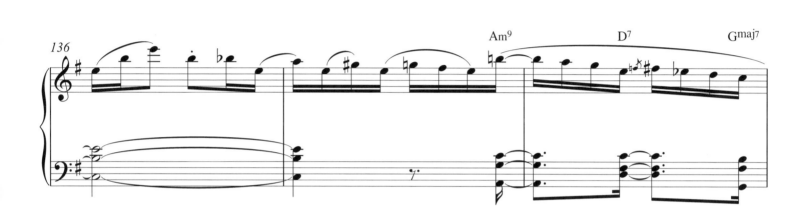

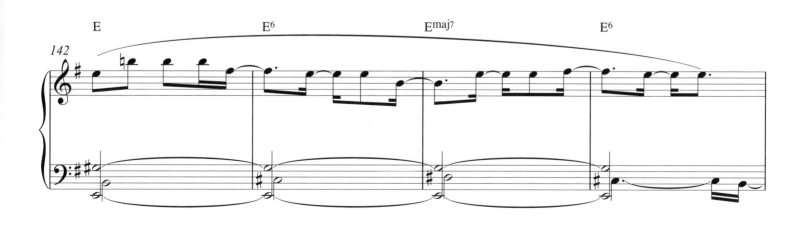

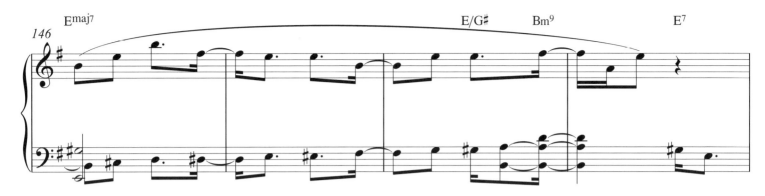

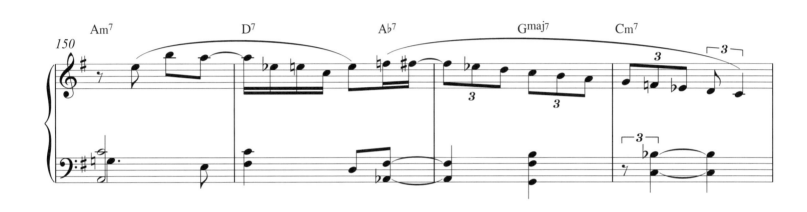

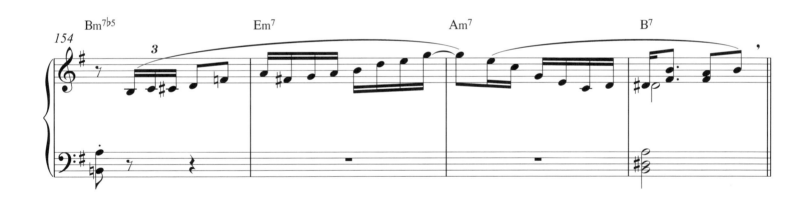

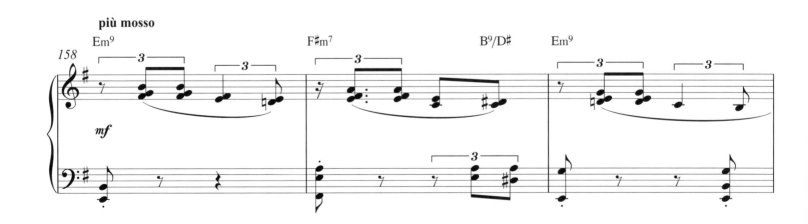

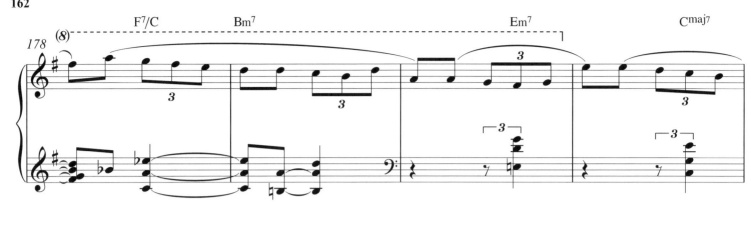

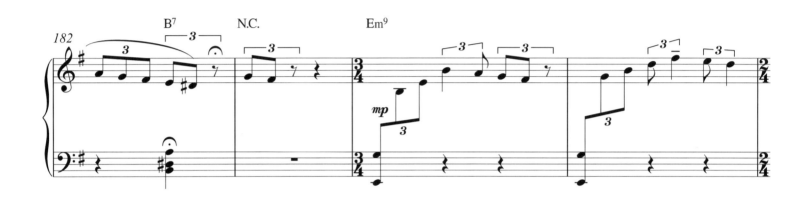

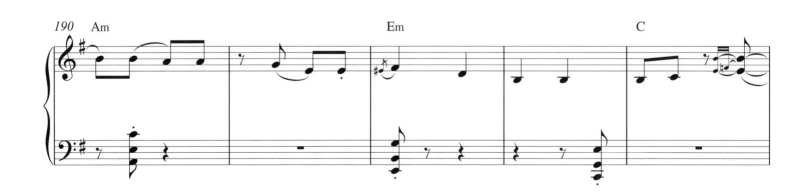

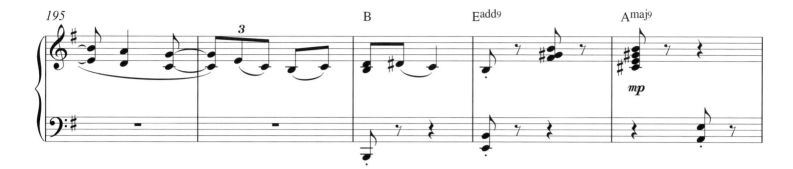

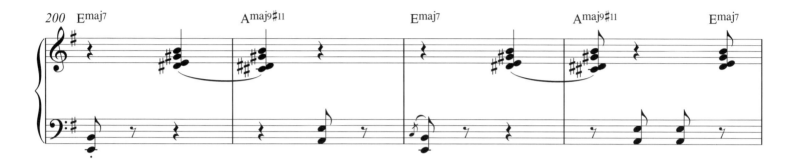

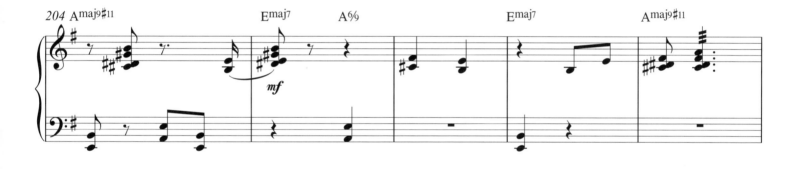

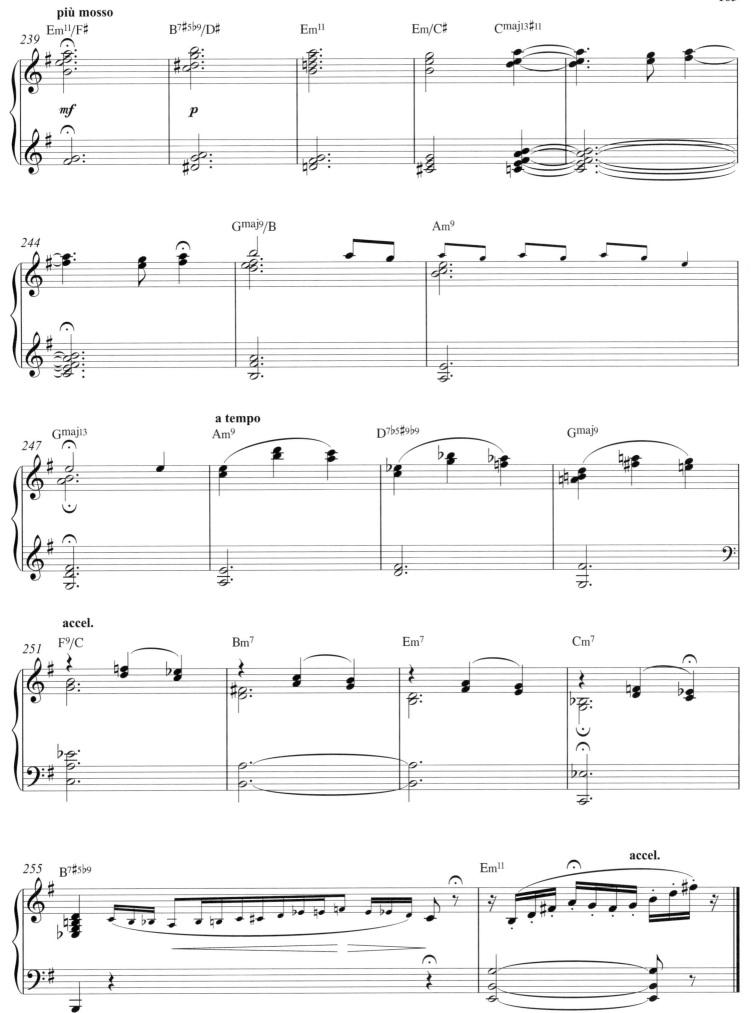

The Nearness Of You

Words by Ned Washington
Music by Hoagy Carmichael

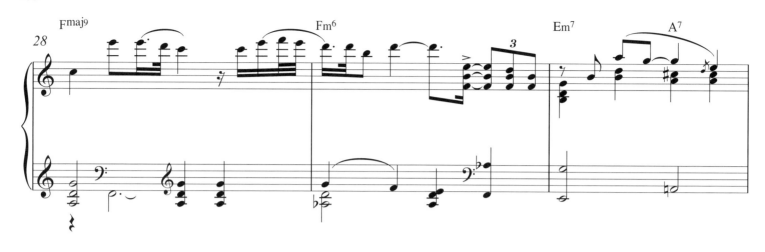

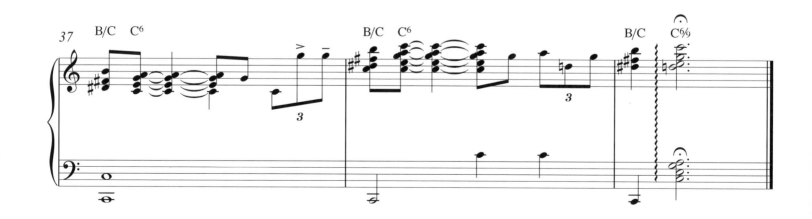

A Night In Tunisia

Music by Dizzy Gillespie & Frank Paparelli

Moderately fast, straight ♩ = 70

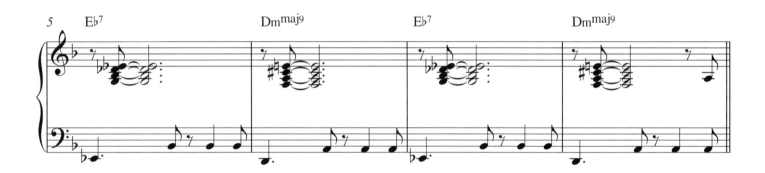

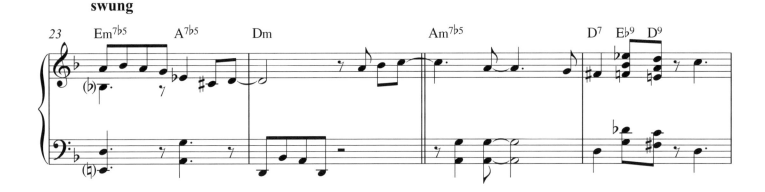

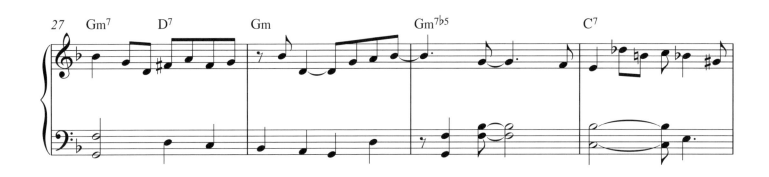

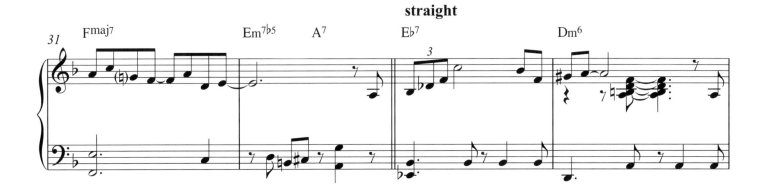

swung

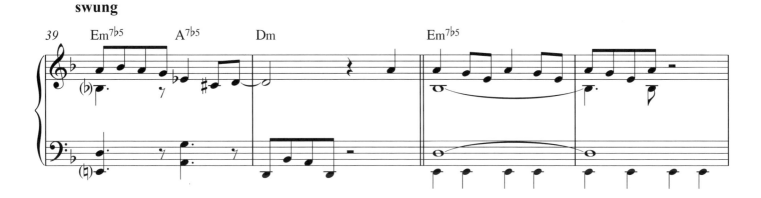

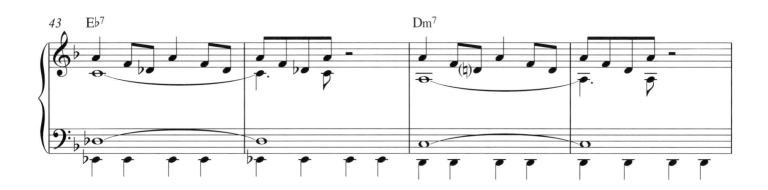

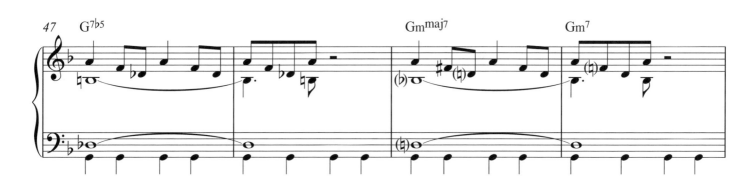

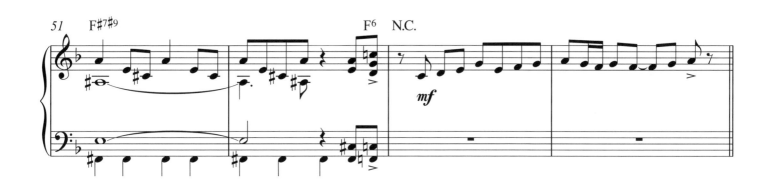

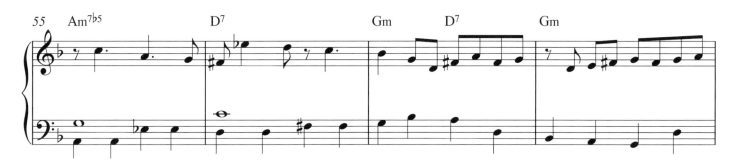

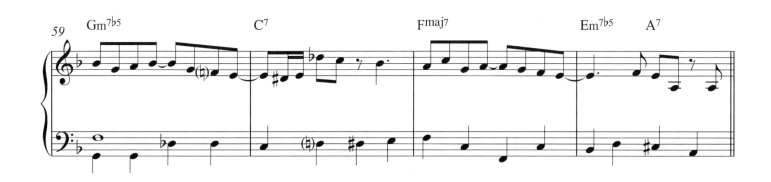

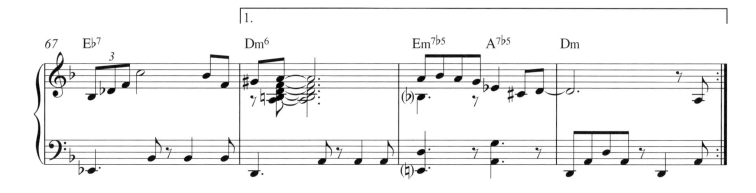

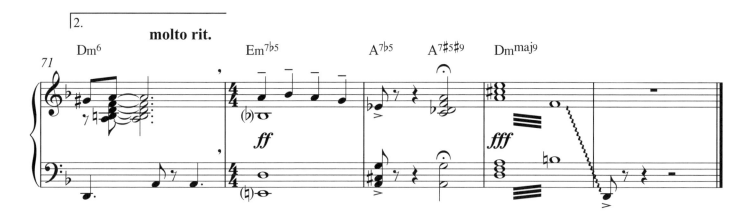

Oleo

Music by Sonny Rollins

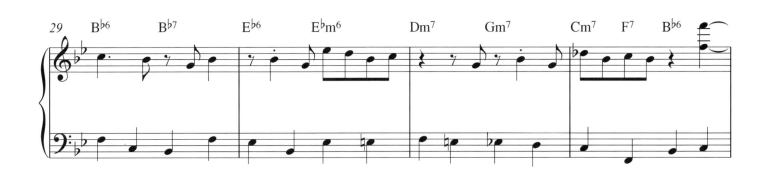

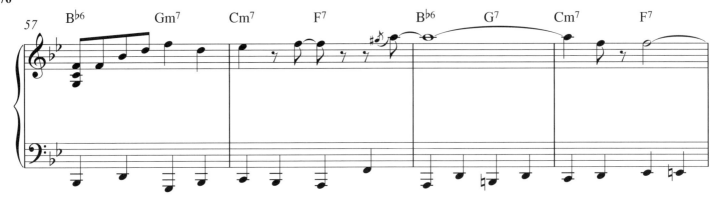

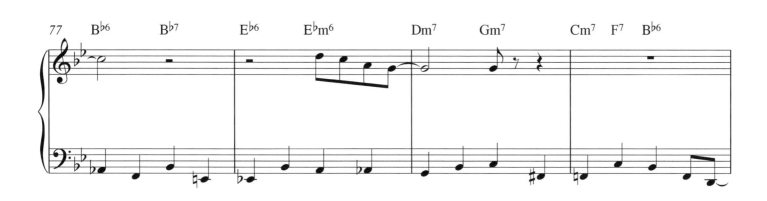

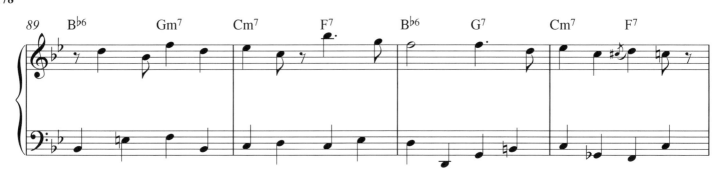

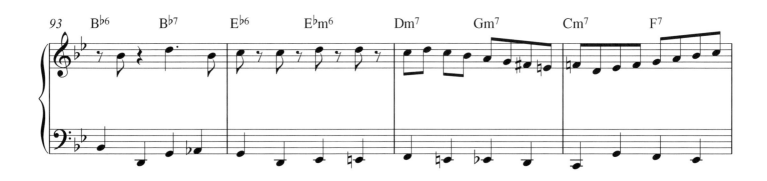

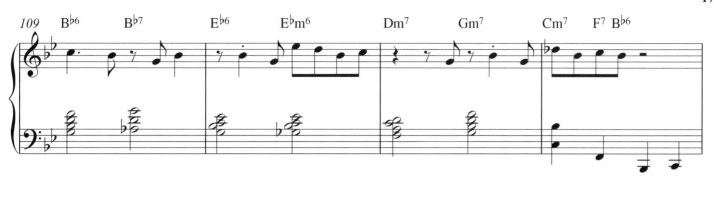

One Note Samba

(Samba De Uma Nota So)

Words by Newton Mendonca
Music by Antonio Carlos Jobim

Medium Bossa nova

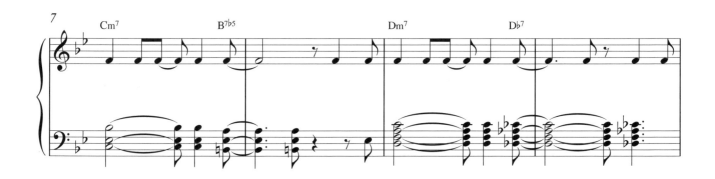

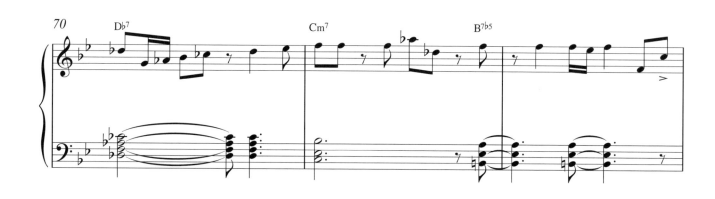

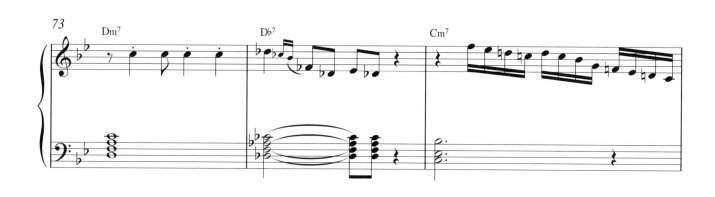

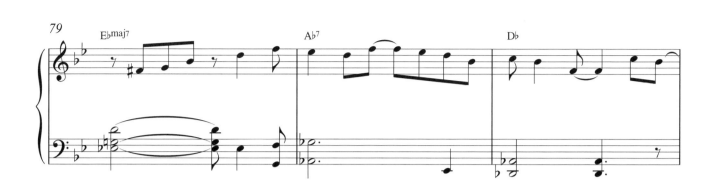

D.S. al Coda

◆ Coda

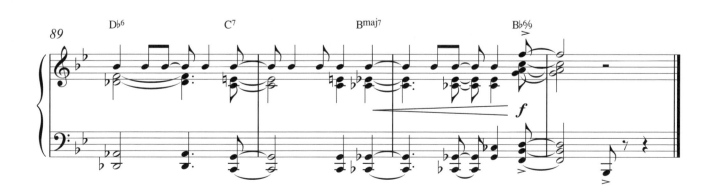

Ornithology

Music by Charlie Parker & Benny Harris

Passion Flower

Music by Billy Strayhorn

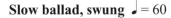

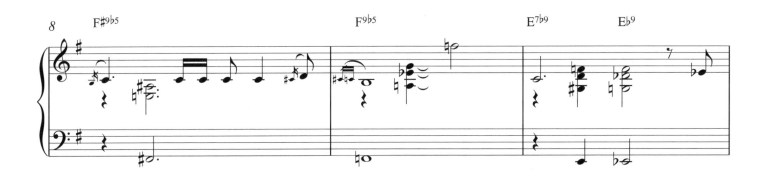

Perdido

Words by Ervin Drake & Harry Lenk
Music by Juan Tizol

Laid-back, swung ♩ = 132

Perhaps, Perhaps, Perhaps

(Quizas, Quizas, Quizas)

Words & Music by Osvaldo Farres
Arranged by Joe Davis

D.S. al Coda

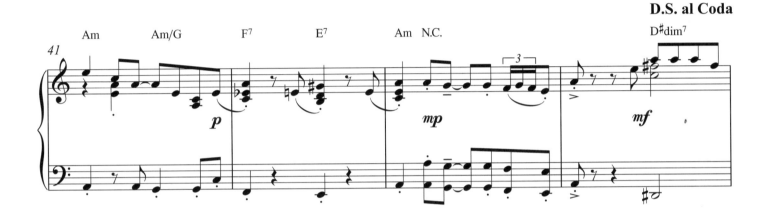

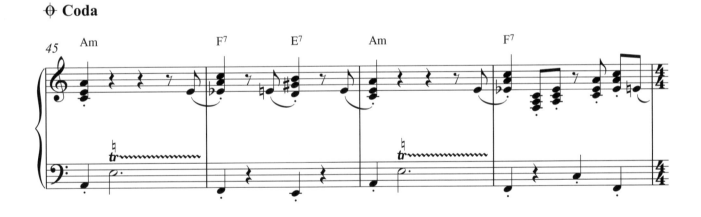

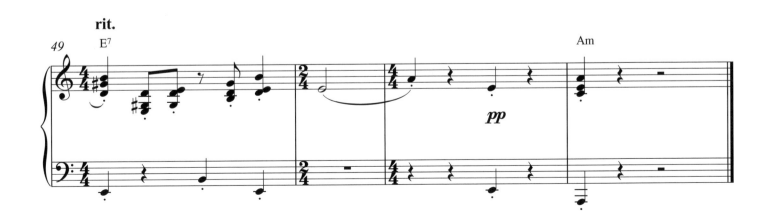

Poinciana

Words by Buddy Bernier
Music by Nat Simon

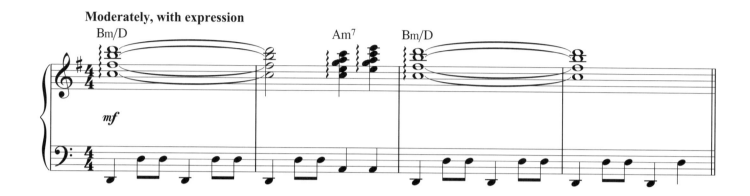

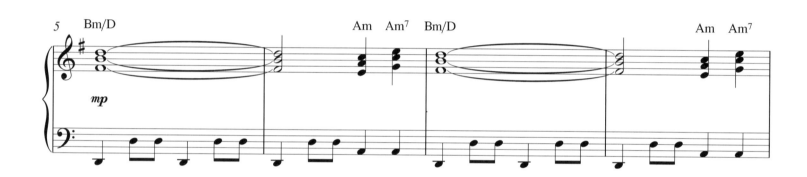

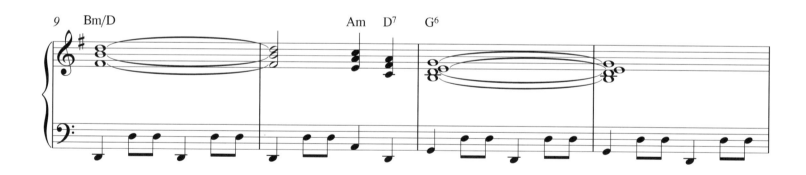

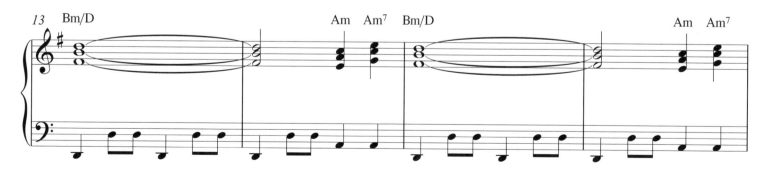

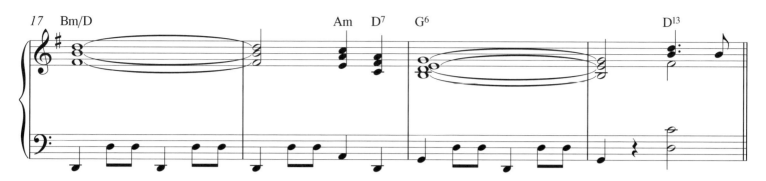

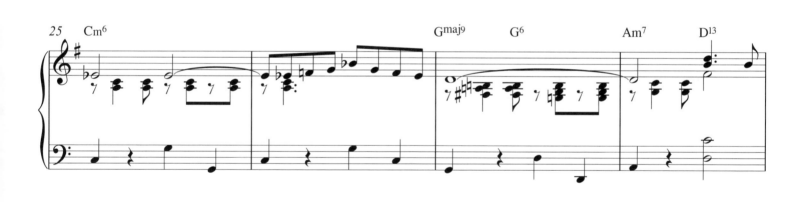

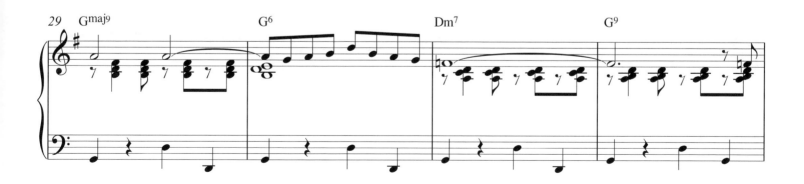

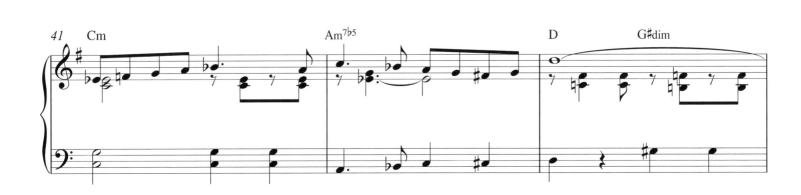

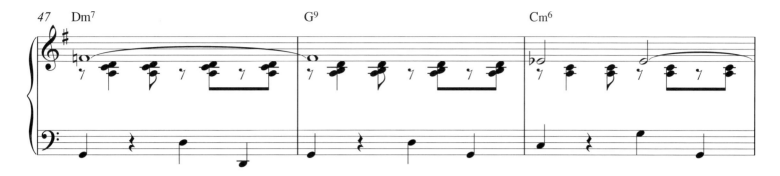

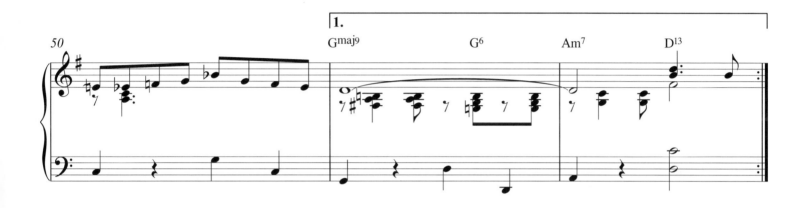

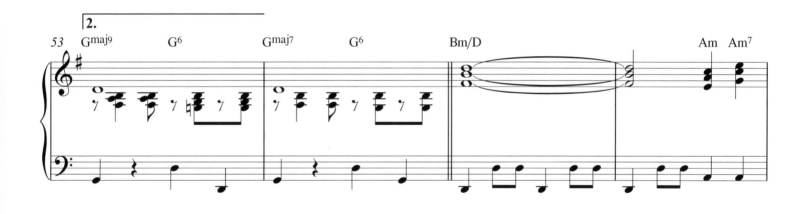

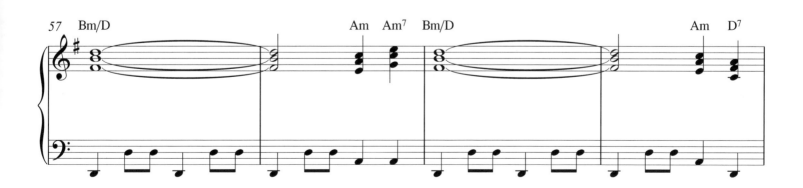

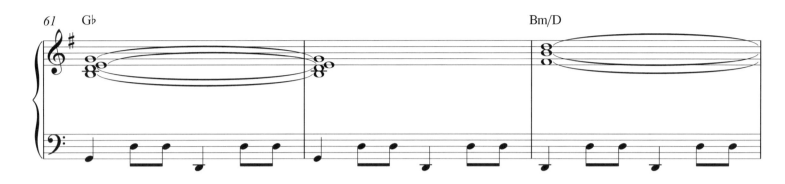

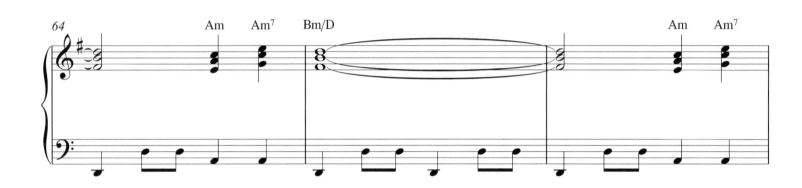

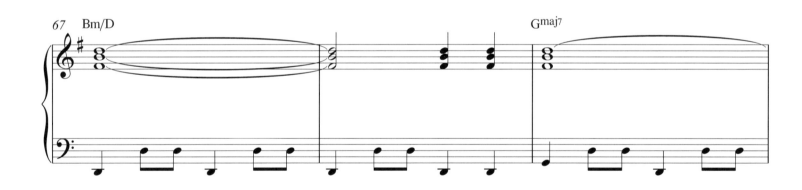

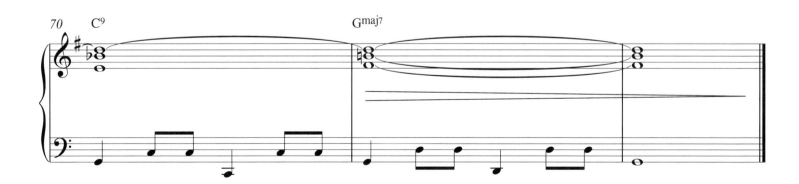

Quiet Now

Words & Music by Denny Zeitlin

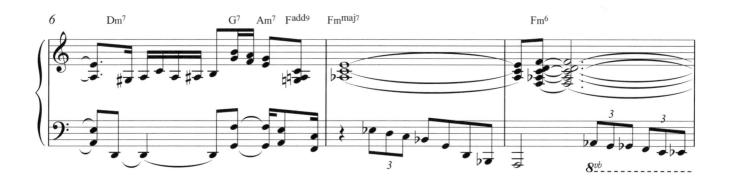

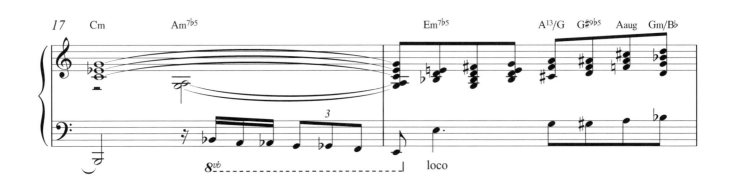

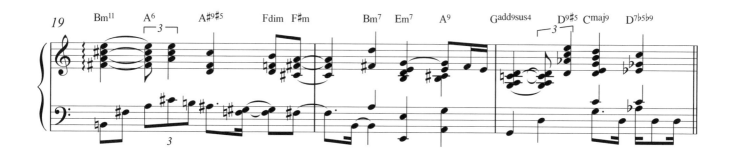

a tempo (medium slow)

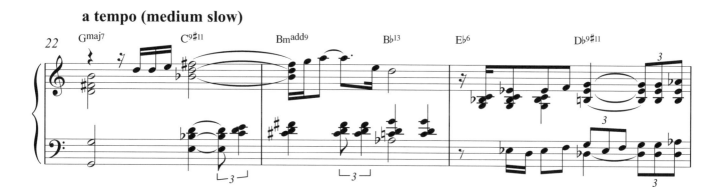

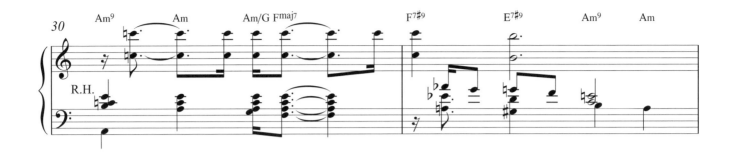

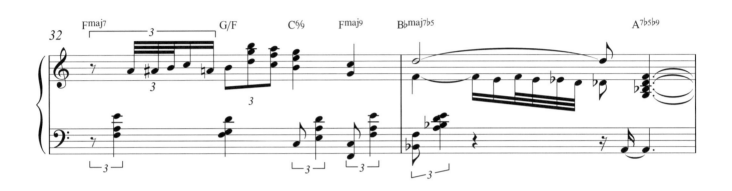

molto rall.

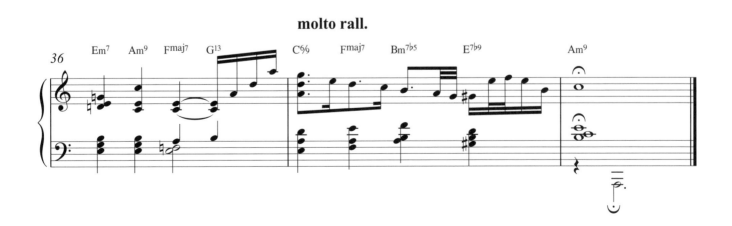

Reflections In D

Words & Music by Edward Ellington

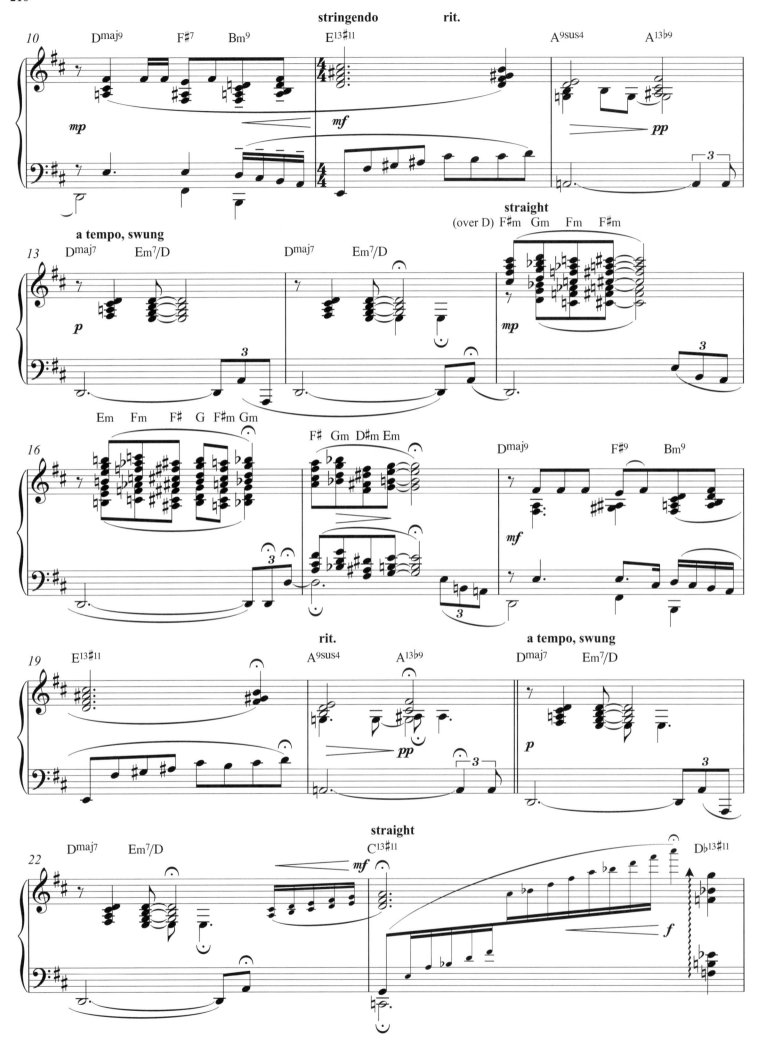

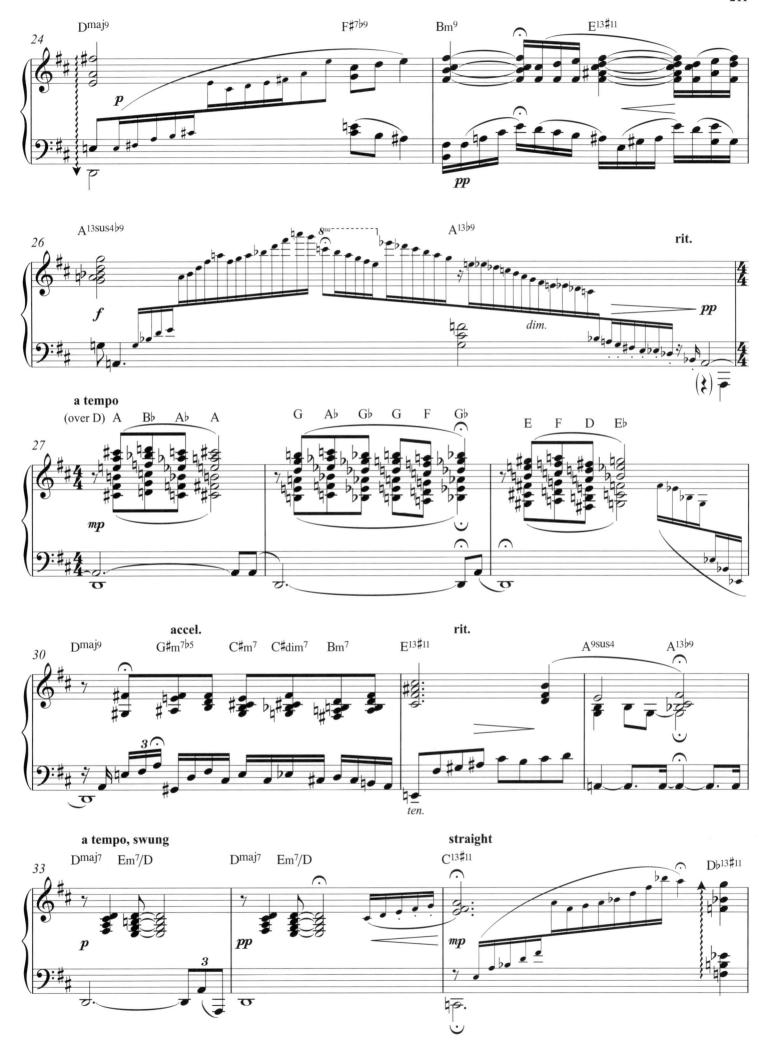

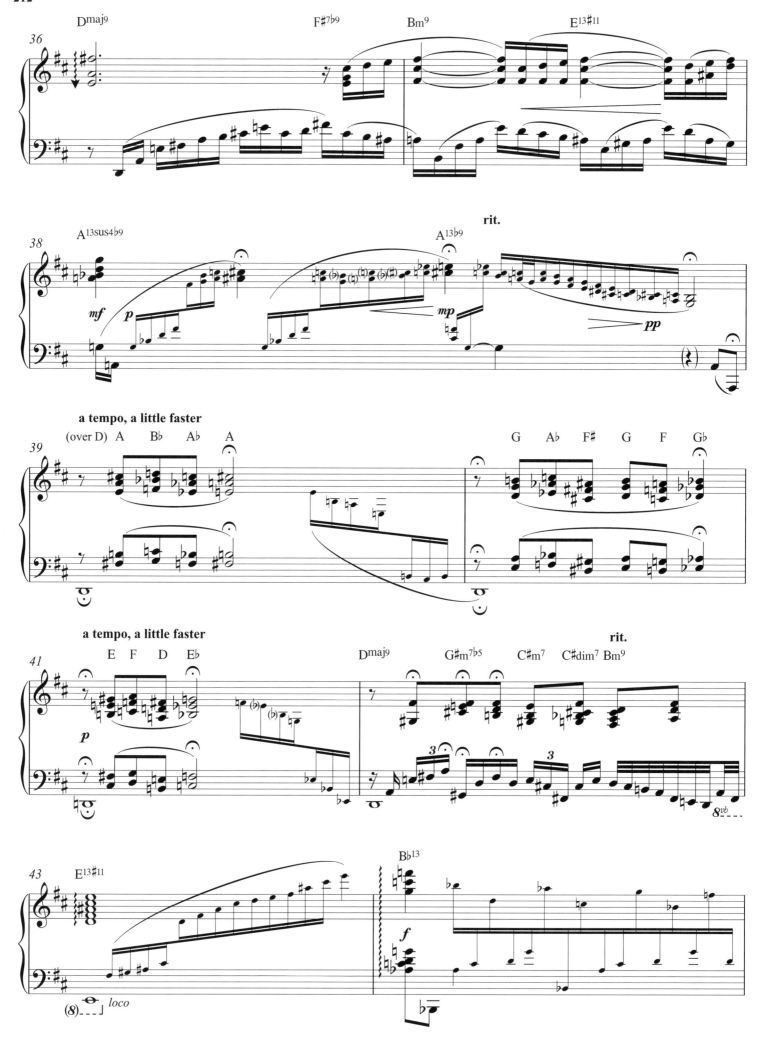

Retrospection

Music by Duke Ellington

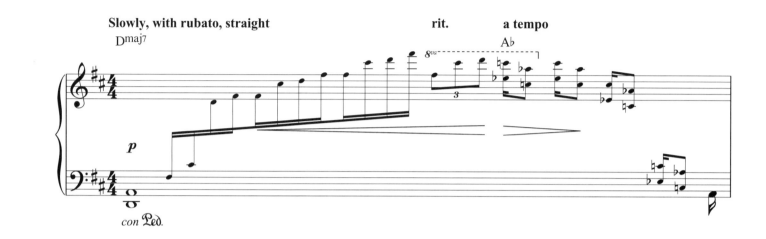

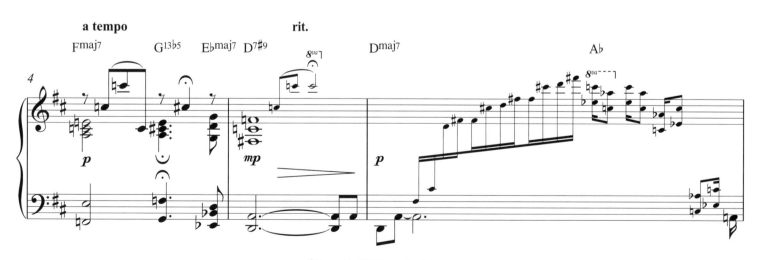

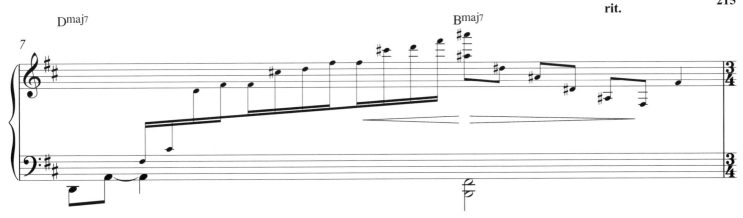

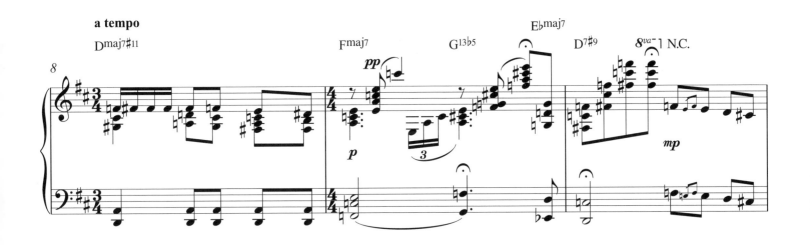

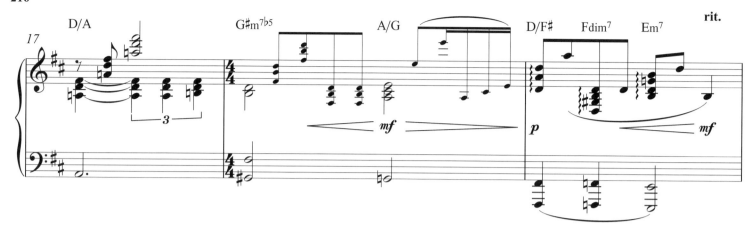

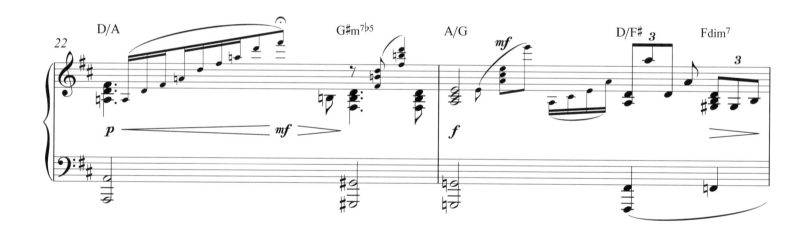

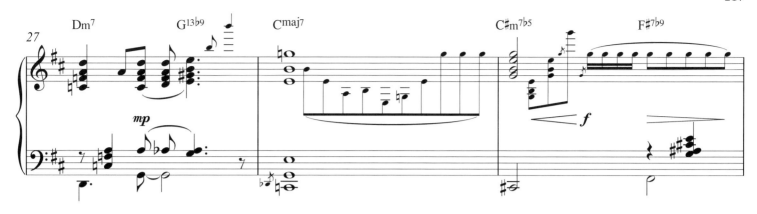

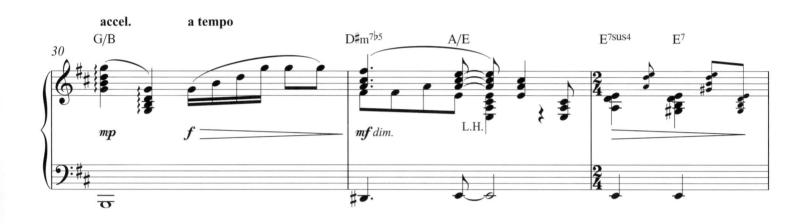

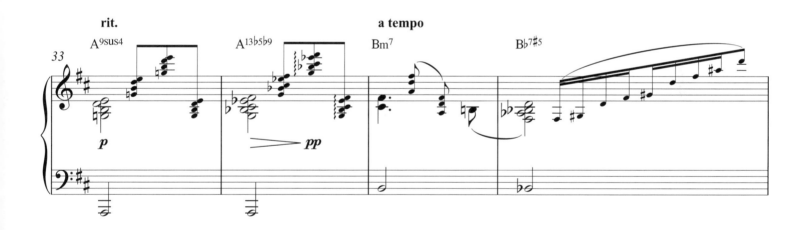

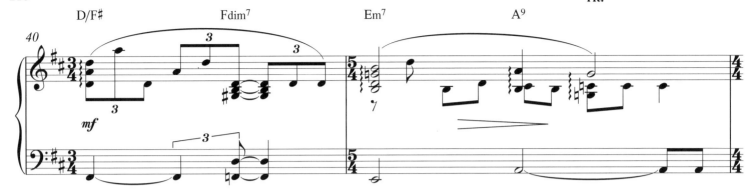

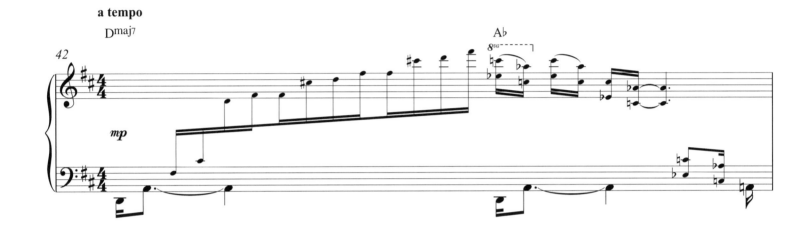

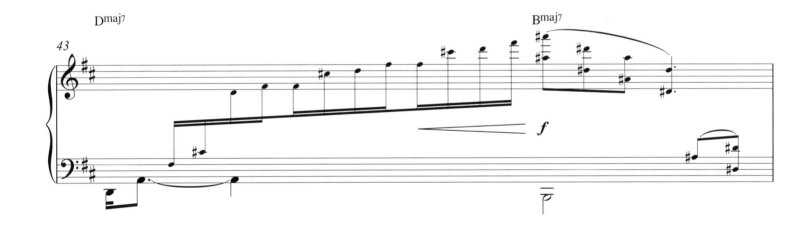

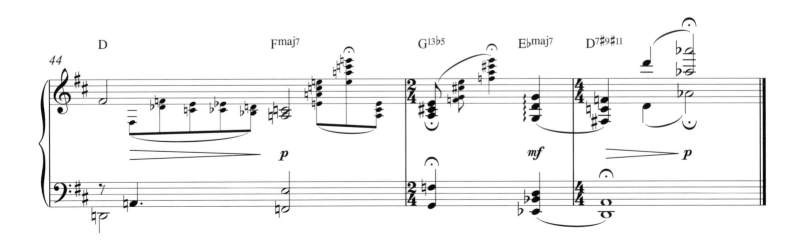

Satin Doll

Words by Johnny Mercer
Music by Duke Ellington & Billy Strayhorn

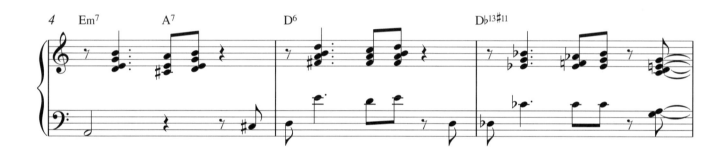

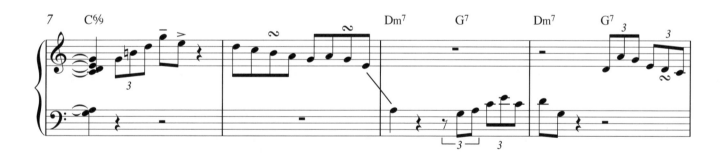

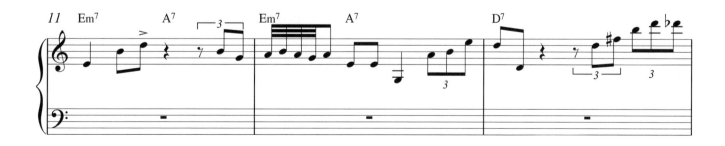

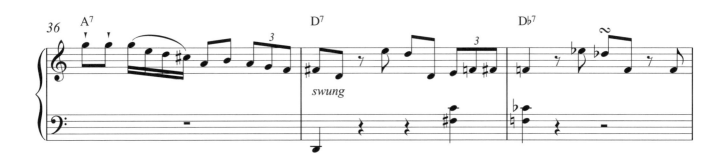

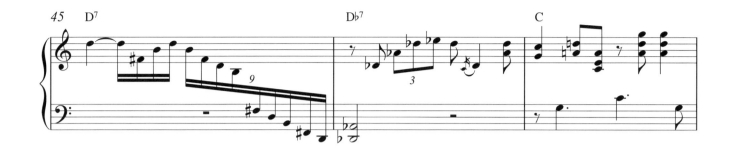

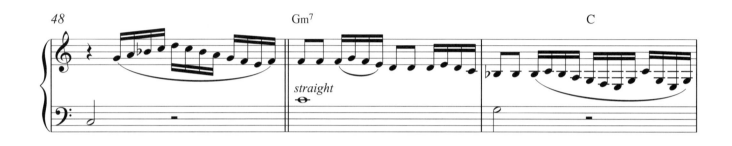

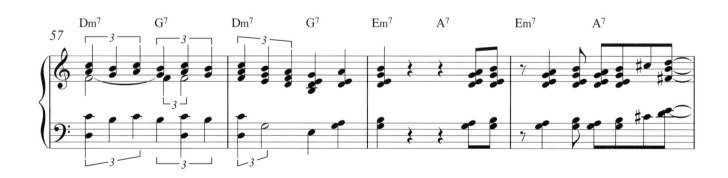

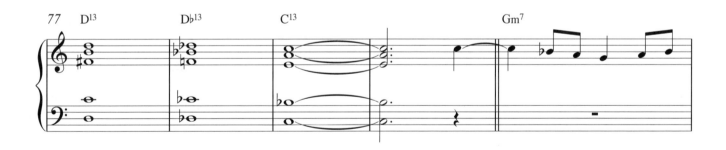

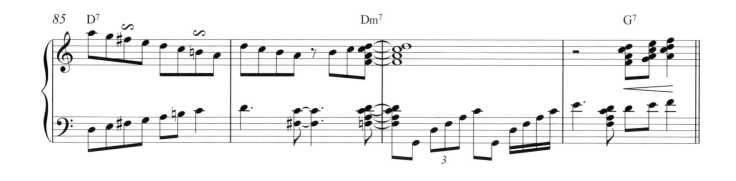

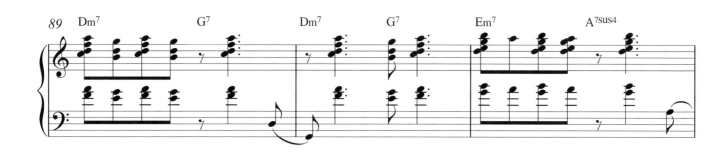

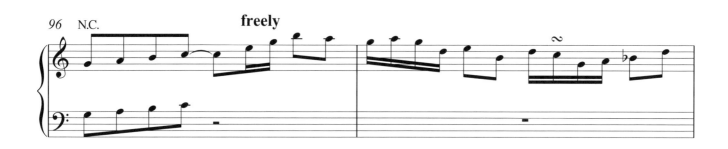

Silence

Music by Charlie Haden

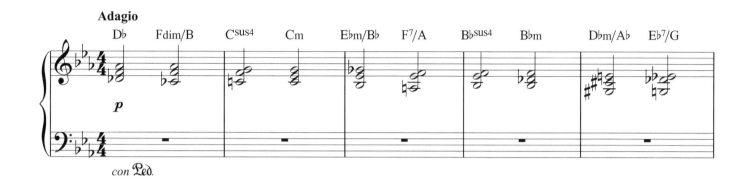

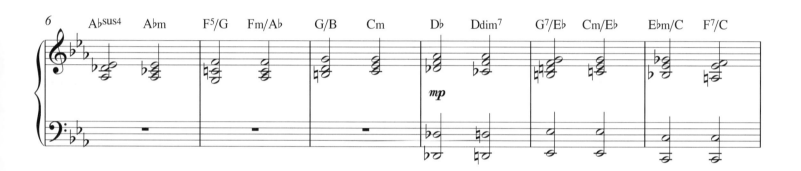

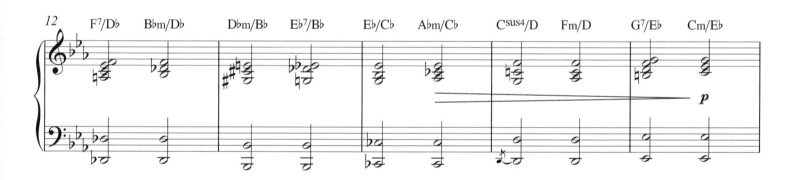

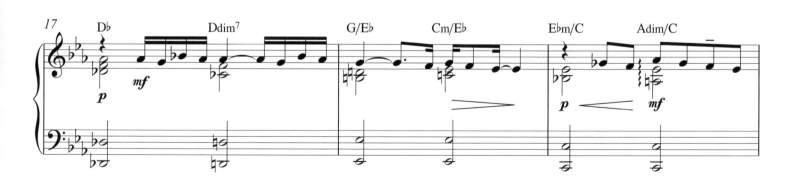

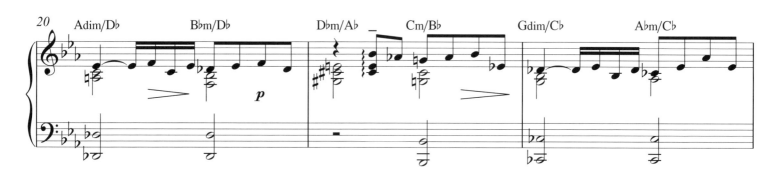

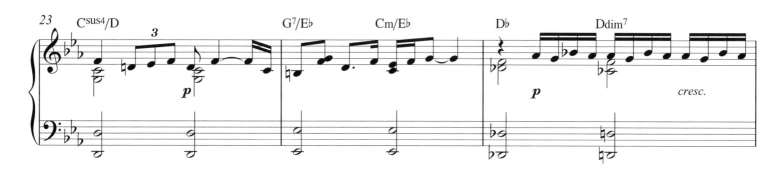

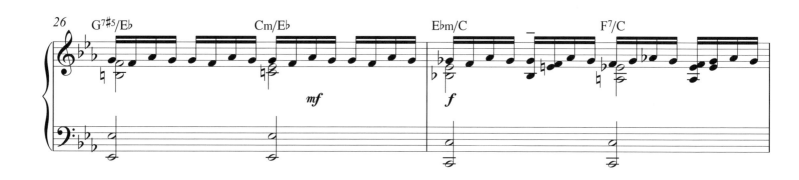

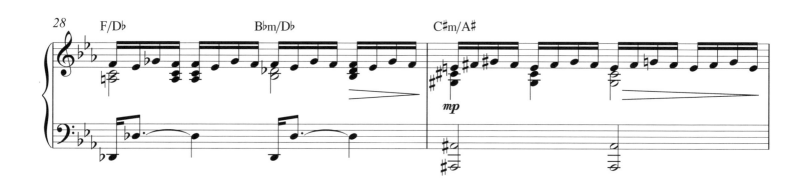

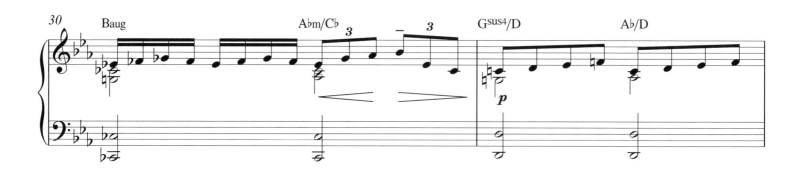

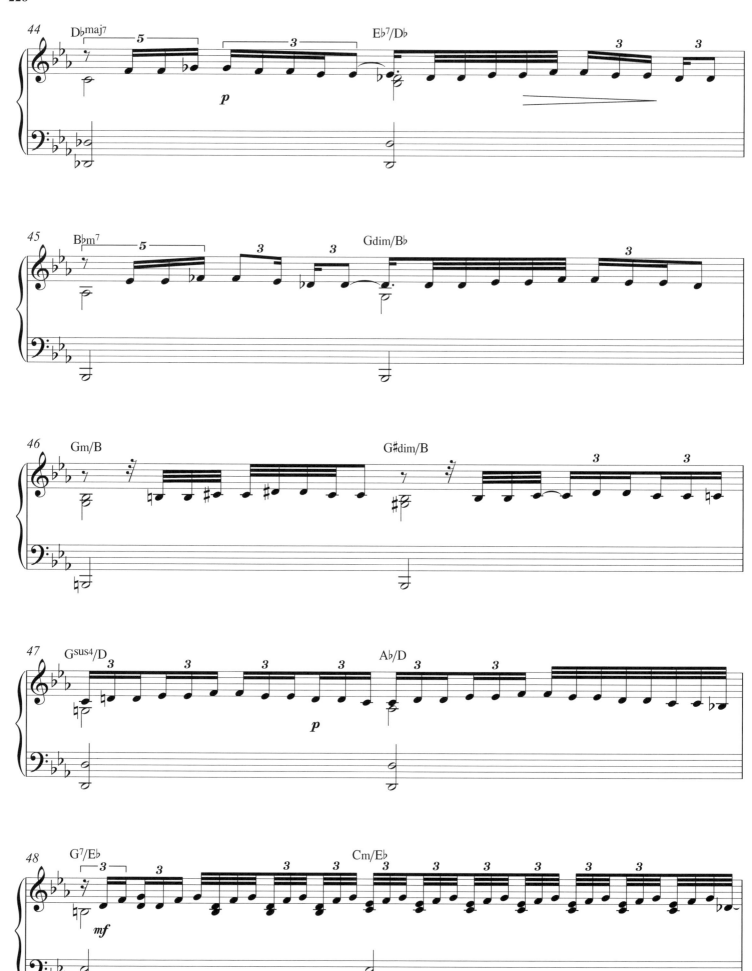

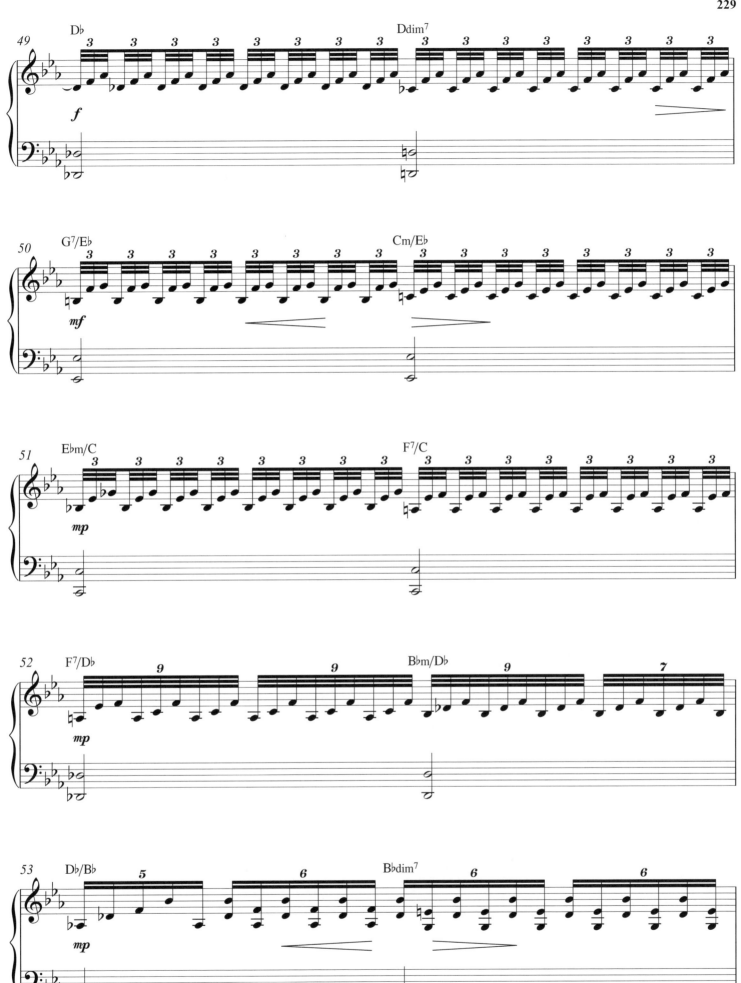

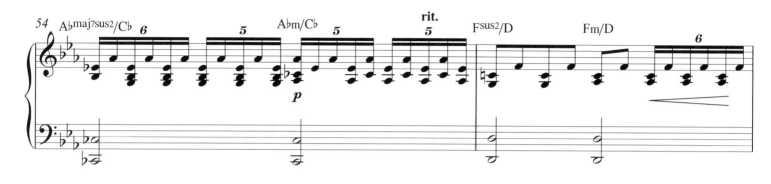

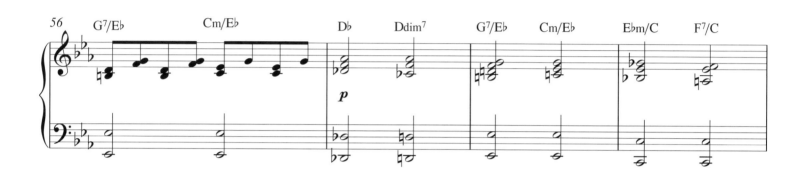

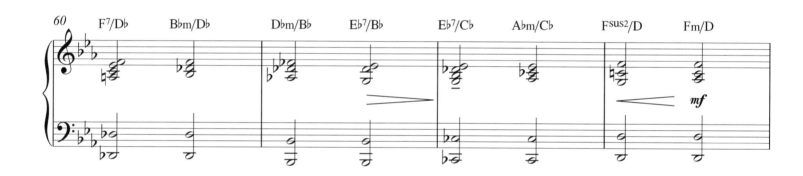

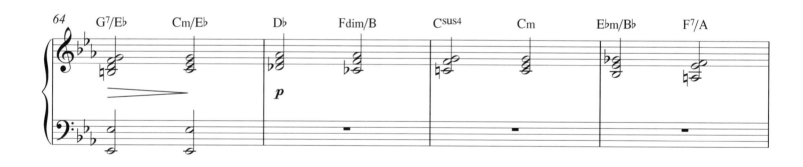

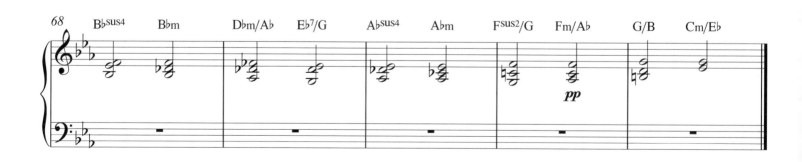

Smoke Gets In Your Eyes

Words by Otto Harbach
Music by Jerome Kern

So Nice
(Summer Samba)

Words by Norman Gimbel & Paulo Sergio Valle

Music by Marcos Valle

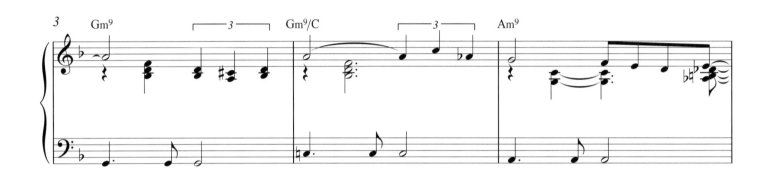

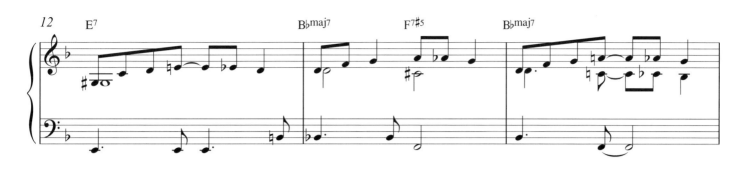

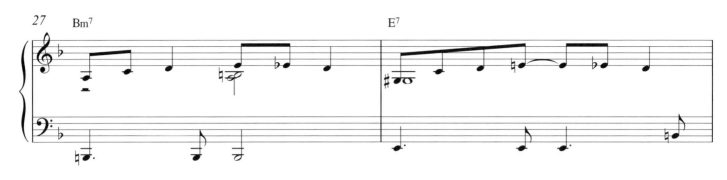

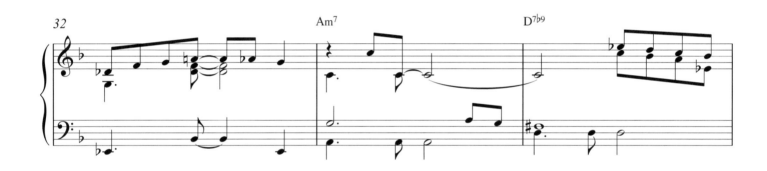

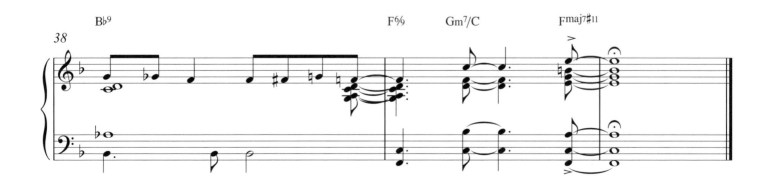

So What

Music by Miles Davis

Explorative ♩ = 60

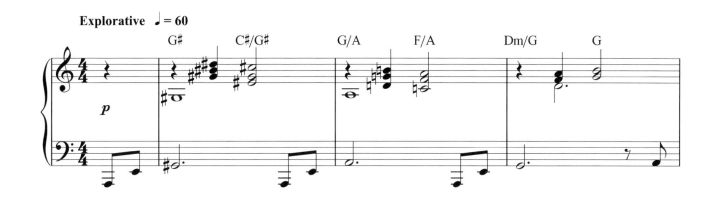

Freely

metric and swung ♩ = 138

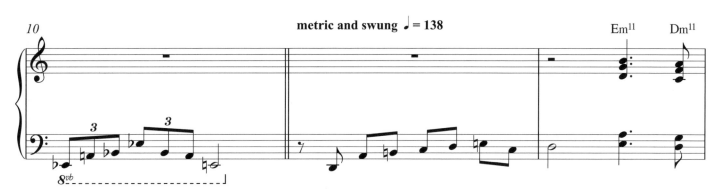

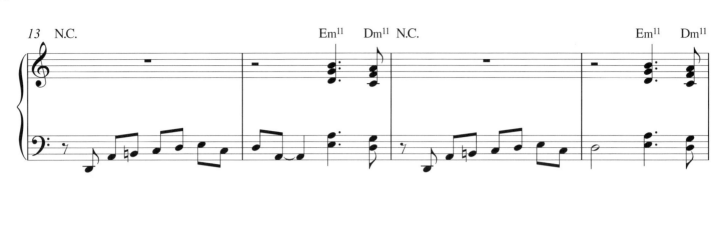

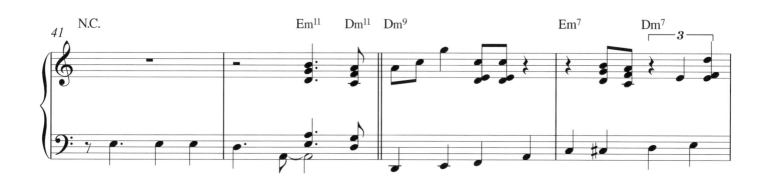

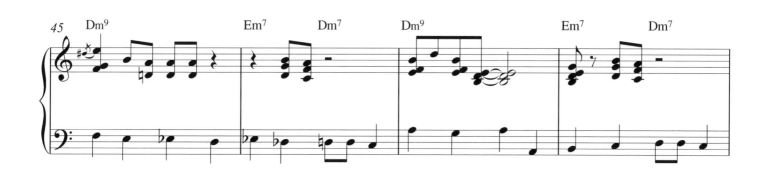

Solitude

Words by Eddie De Lange & Irving Mills
Music by Duke Ellington

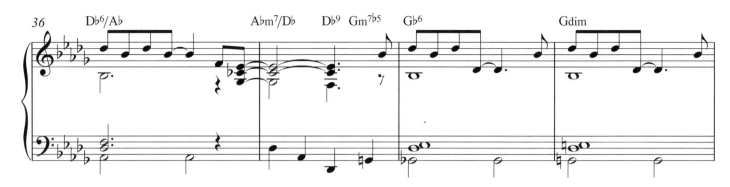

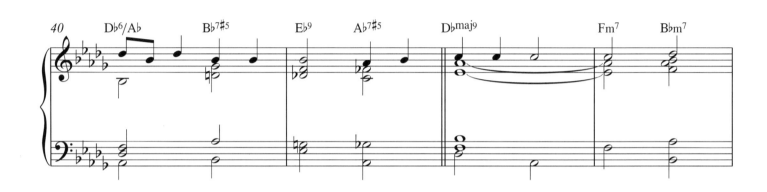

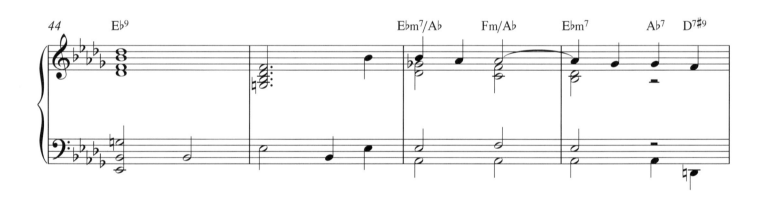

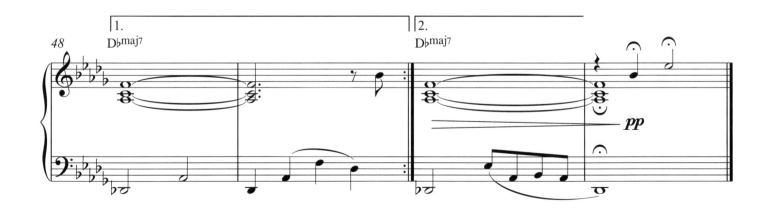

Stardust

Words by Mitchell Parish
Music by Hoagy Carmichael

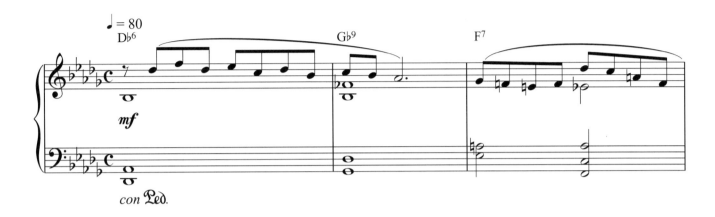

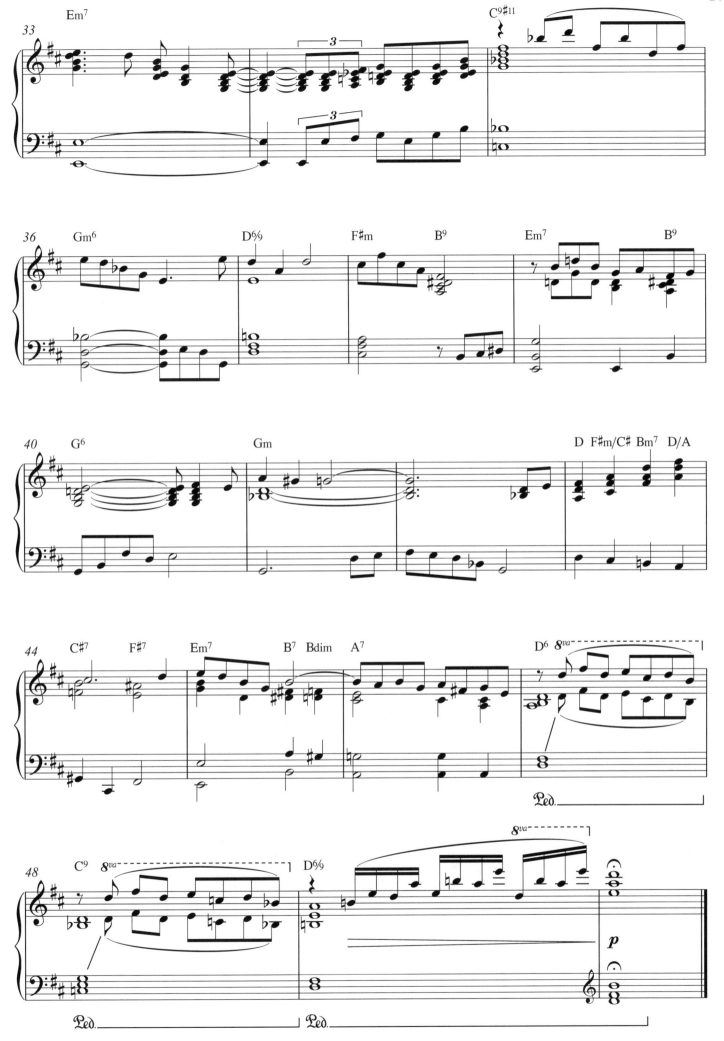

Struttin' With Some Barbecue

Words by Don Raye
Music by Louis Armstrong

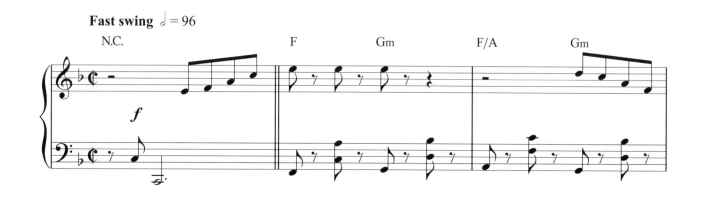

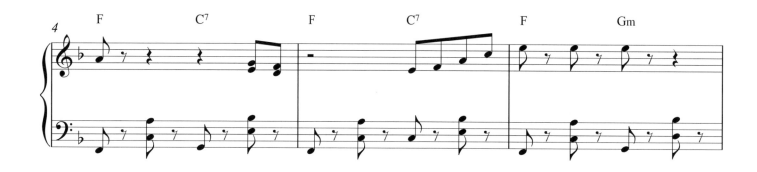

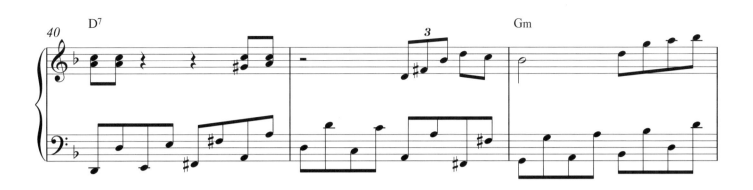

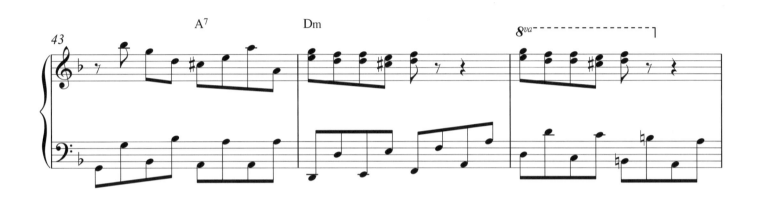

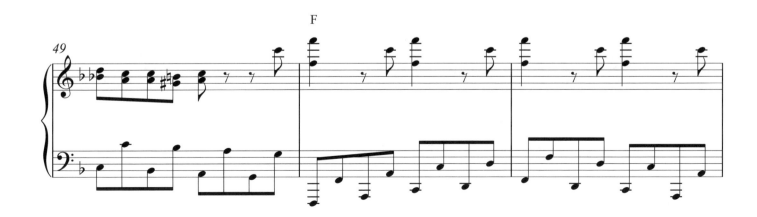

Sway

(Quien Sera)

Words & Music by Pablo Beltran Ruiz & Luis Demetrio Traconis Molina
English Lyrics by Norman Gimbel

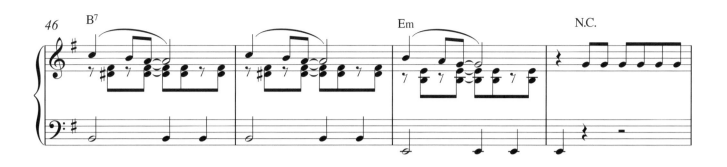

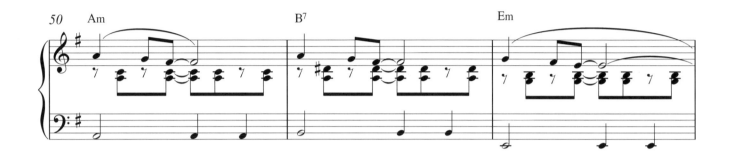

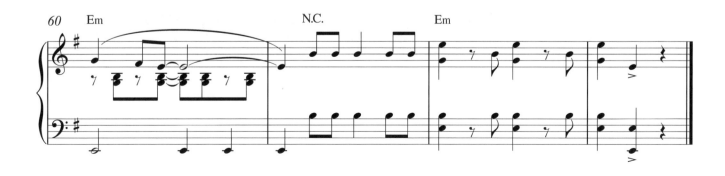

Take The 'A' Train

Words & Music by Billy Strayhorn

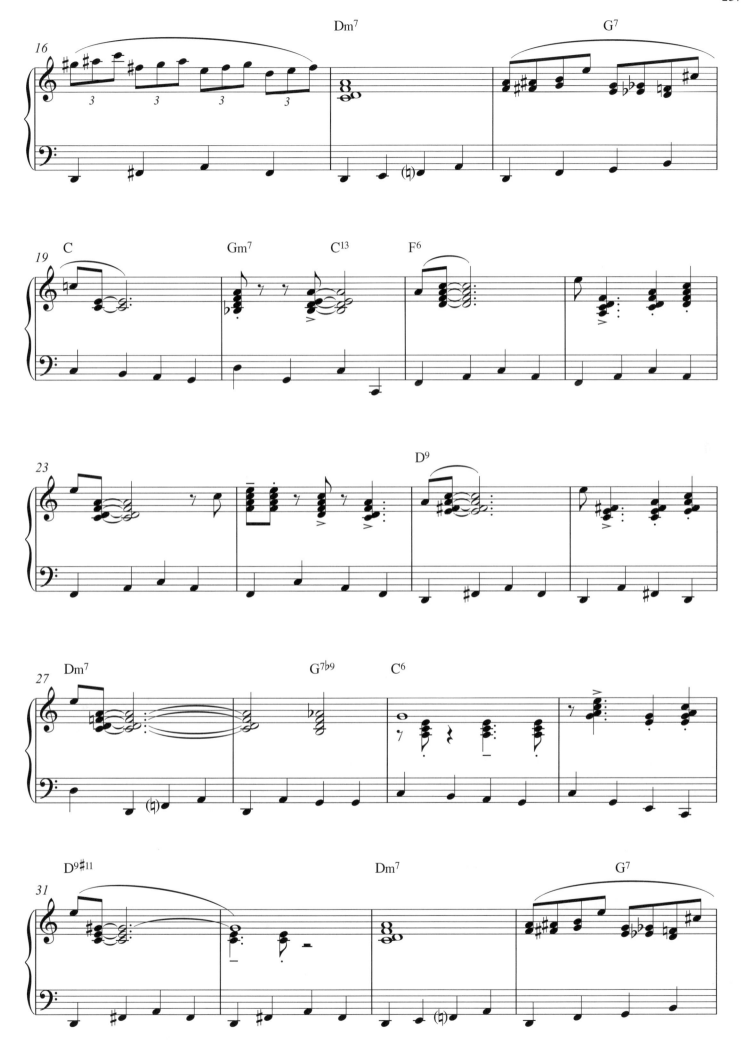

The Very Thought Of You

Words & Music by Ray Noble

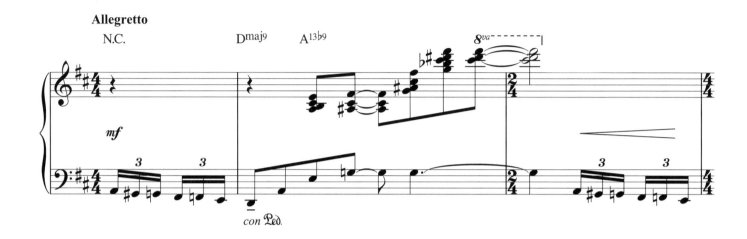

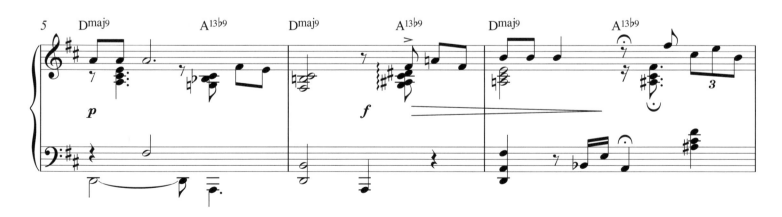

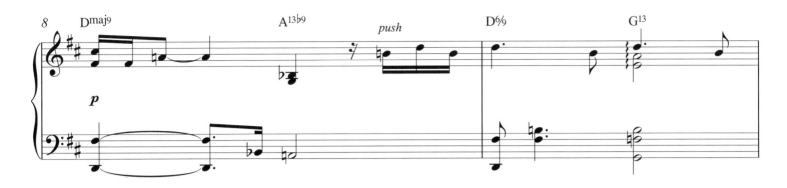

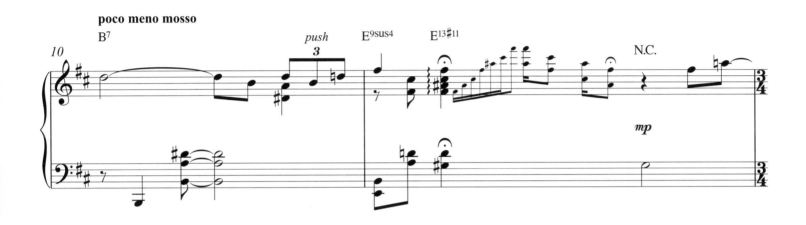

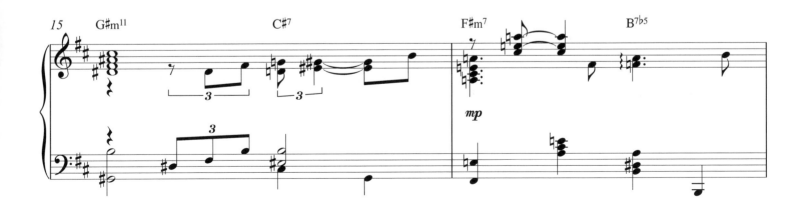

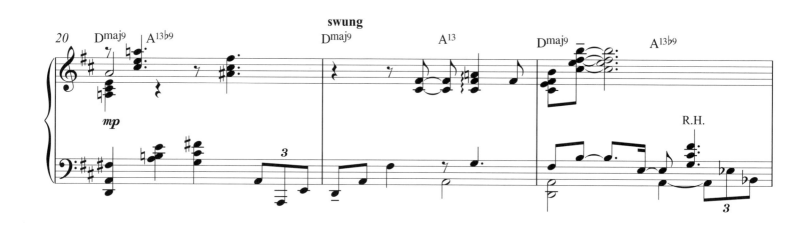

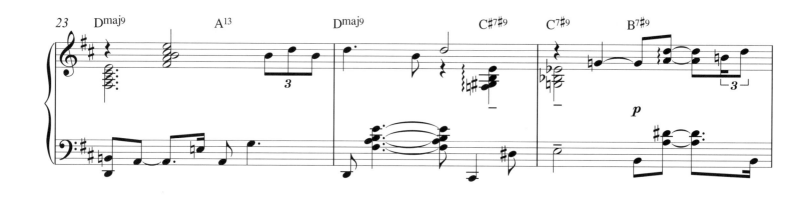

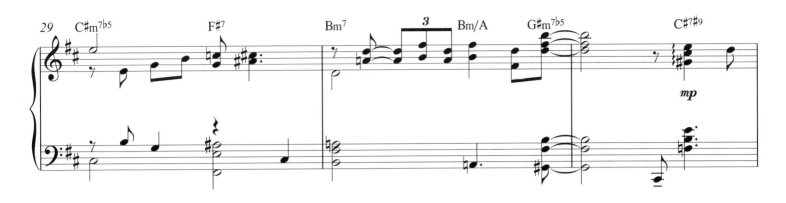

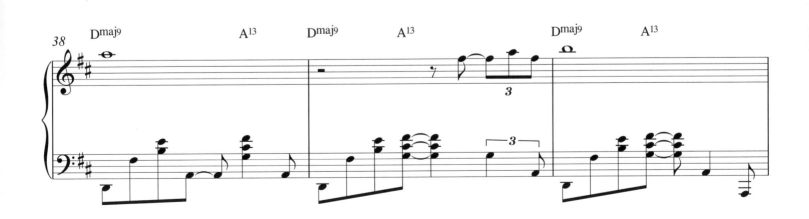

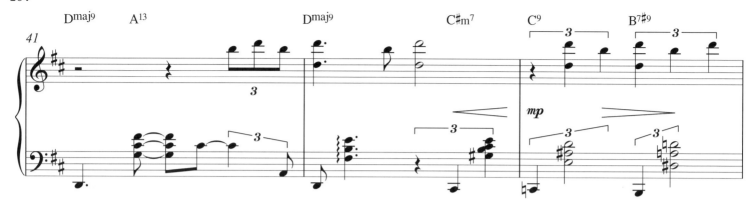

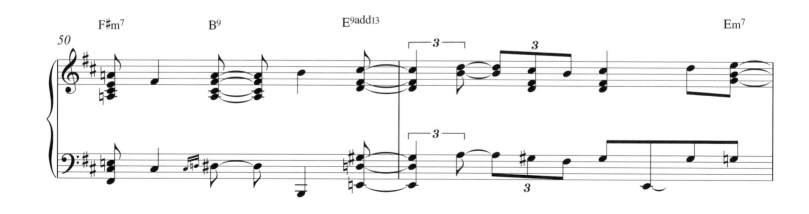

Two Lonely People

Words & Music by Bill Evans

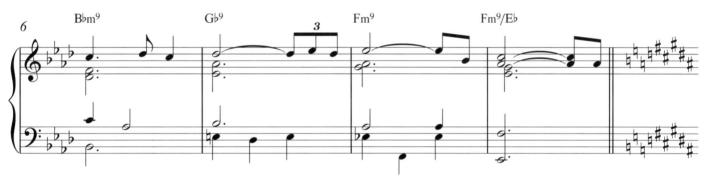

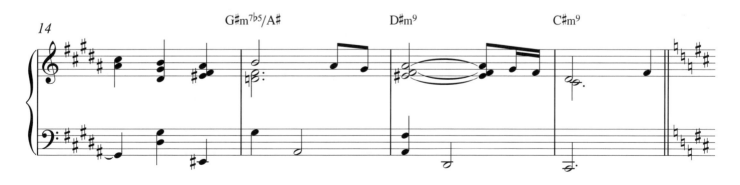

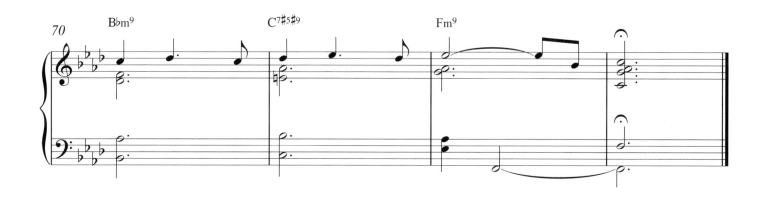

Waltz For Debby

Words by Gene Lees
Music by Bill Evans

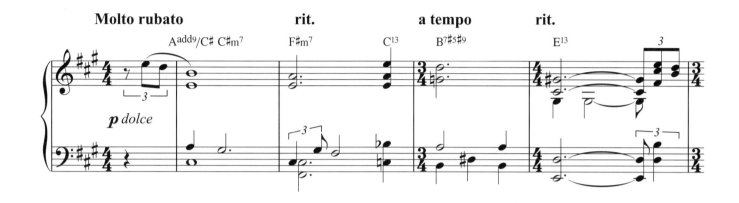

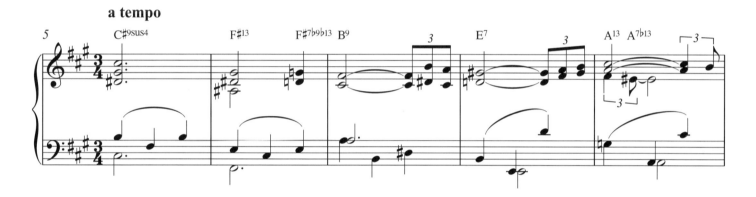

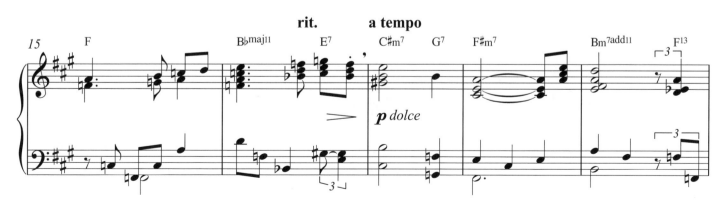

272

The Way You Look Tonight

Words by Dorothy Fields
Music by Jerome Kern

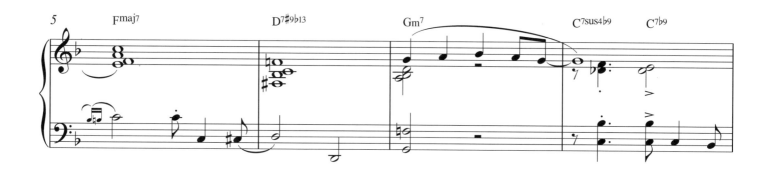

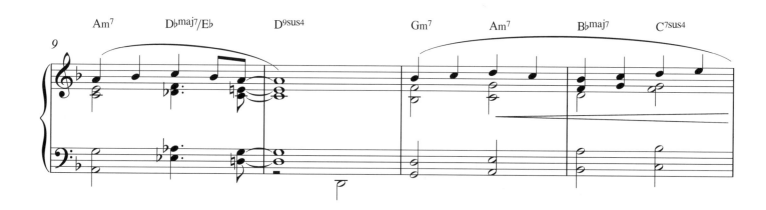

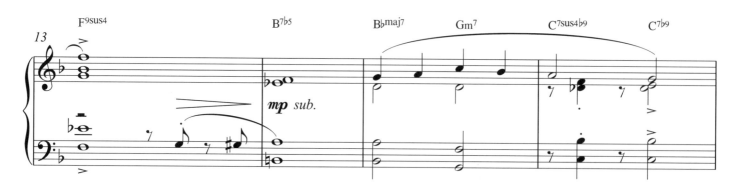

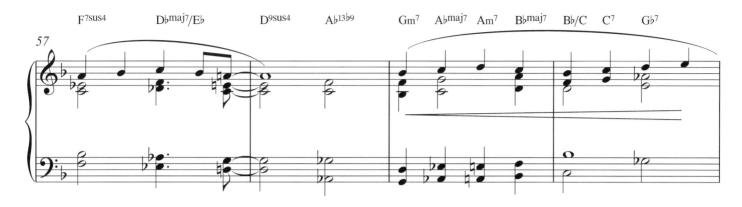

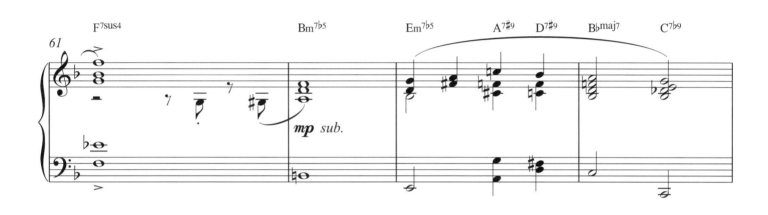

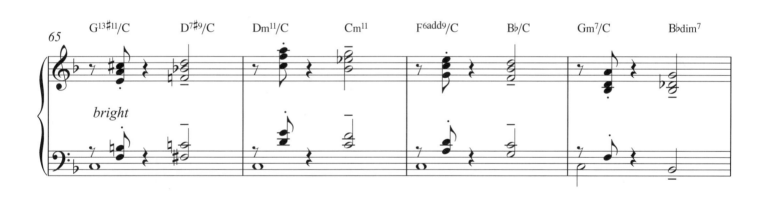

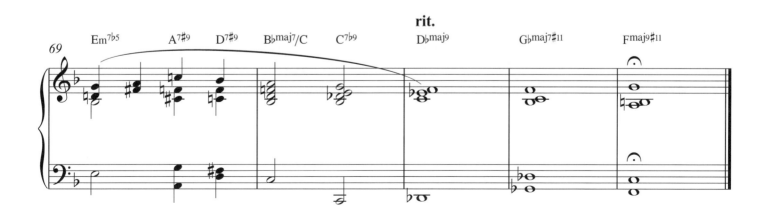

When Sunny Gets Blue

Words by Jack Segal
Music by Marvin Fisher

Moderately slow

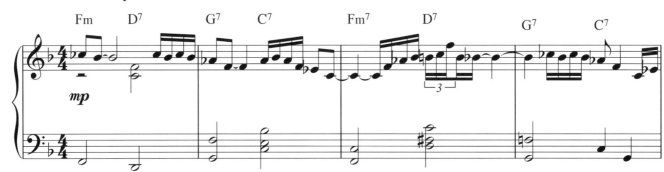

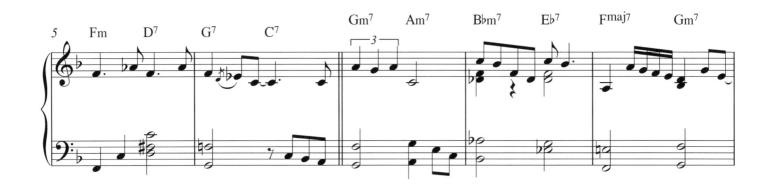

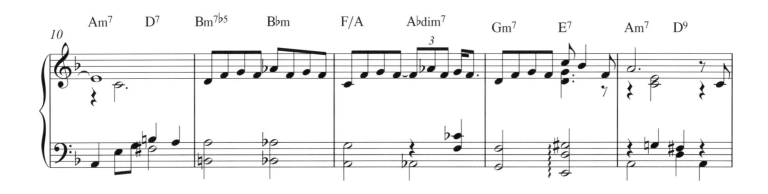

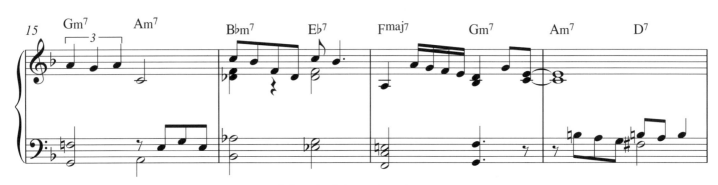

Your Love Has Faded

Words & Music by Duke Ellington & Billy Strayhorn

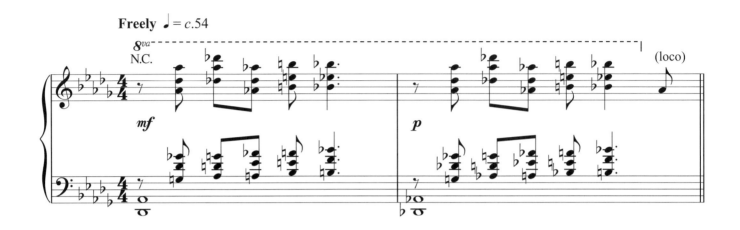

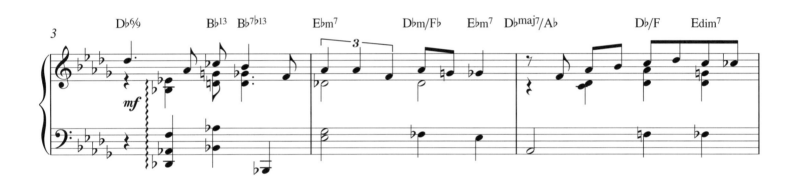

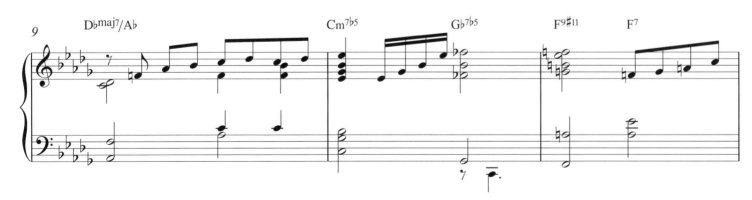